天下

龍泉

天下龙泉

龙泉青瓷与全球化

卷四　交融辉映

故宫博物院、浙江省博物馆、丽水市人民政府 编

故宫出版社

Longquan of the World

Longquan Celadon and Globalization

Vol. Ⅳ
Imitations and Evolvements

Compiled by the Palace Museum, the Zhejiang Provincial Museum and the Lishui Municipal People's Government

The Forbidden City Publishing House

目 录

Contents

序一

丝绸之路由众多不同的主干道和无数的支线组成，是在亚洲、欧洲和东非、北非乃至撒哈拉以南非洲的部分国家和地区之间构建起来的一个海陆交通网络。虽然不同国家、民族对历史上曾加入的这个交通网络有着不同的命名，但是作为连接东方和西方的干道，丝绸之路有机地把东亚、南亚、中亚、西亚、北非、东非和欧洲的主要文明古国连接在了一起。对比构成丝绸之路的网线与当今“一带一路”倡议所覆盖的路线，会发现二者之间有着极大的契合度，这说明丝绸之路不仅曾经沟通、连接着古代世界，也是当代世界交通网线的前身，更是一条贯通古今、连接各文明区域经济、文化、政治、军事的交流之路。

在历史的长河中，丝绸之路上既有在东西方不同地区之间进行交换的商品，也有为了政治、宗教、商业或军事等各种目的而行进在丝路上的人群。正是这些商品和人群的流动，让古代的人们了解到在自身文明之外还有其他的文明，他们用各自的语言记录下了对自己域外文明的认识。这些零星的记载，成了古代世界史的一部分，是今人了解古代、研究世界古代文明的重要资料。人群的流动带来了各种宗教与思想在东西方之间的传播，在宗教思想影响下的宗教艺术也同时得到了普及。对来自异域产品的渴求与模仿，则促成了技术在东西方不同地区之间的传播与互动，带动了技术水平的共同提升，促进着人类文明的交融发展。

正是得益于丝绸之路，古代的各国家、地区和文明区域才得以被连接起来。由此，在不同历史时期内，各个国家与文明之间才有可能在继承与发展自身传统文化的同时，不断吸纳和包容外来文化因素，并在这个过程中变得开放、强大。是故，丝绸之路的历史价值也越来越受到重视，继陆上的“丝绸之路：长安—天山廊道的路网”被列入《世界遗产名录》之后，“海上丝绸之路”的申遗工作也在进行之中。同时，对丝绸之路的研究也是海内外学术界共同关心的重要课题。

利用文物展览的方式，更大范围、更深层次地揭示和宣传丝绸之路的历史价值，也是各博物馆工作中一个重要的努力方向。在关注通过丝绸之路流入中国的异域文物，以及在外来文明、技术影响下的本地产品的同时，如何使展览不只停留在物的层面，而能通过文物展览更好地叙述因交流而在不同文明之间产生的相互影响，以及技术水平共同提高的历史真实，应该是策展人员要进一步思考和关注的内容，也是文物展览所要体现的更高境界。故宫博物院一向注重以学术研究为基础进行展览策划，此次故宫博物院联合浙江省博物馆、丽水市人民政府共同举办的“天下龙泉——龙泉青瓷与全球化”展览，就是我院与浙江省博物馆的陶瓷研究人员在联合承担国家文物局指南针计划 2012 ~ 2014 年“中国古代瓷器生产技术对外传播研究”课题的成果，但展览又不局限于课题本身，而是以龙泉青瓷和龙泉青瓷所代表的瓷器生产技术、文化为切入点，思考在 12 ~ 15 世纪、在新航路开辟前，在世界范围内龙泉青瓷广泛流布的表象背后，对各国、各地区陶瓷器生产技术的影响。通过观察越南、泰国、日本和英国等国对龙泉青瓷的完全仿烧，以及缅甸、伊朗、叙利亚、埃及等国利用本地传统的陶瓷生产技术仿烧龙泉青瓷的情况，进而指出各地的仿烧虽有表现形式上的差别，但本质上却无一不是通过文化与技术交融，实现各地陶瓷技术的共同提高，龙泉青瓷也因之具有了世界性。对龙泉青瓷的渴求和仿烧，也成为促成早期全球化的动因之一。

感谢北京故宫文物保护基金会、龙湖集团、浙江省博物馆、丽水市人民政府对展览工作的大力支持，感谢海内外四十余家博物馆、考古单位和院校对展览的支持和帮助。耿宝昌先生和本院众多同仁为本次展览付出了巨大的努力，在此一并致谢。

是为序！

故宫博物院院长

Preface I

The term Silk Roads refers to the overland and maritime networks of transportation between the countries and regions of Asia, Europe, East Africa, North Africa, and parts of Africa south of the Sahara Desert. The Silk Roads consisted of numerous primary routes and a large number of secondary routes that connected the major countries of East Asia, South Asia, Central Asia, West Asia, North and East Africa and Europe. These regions had their own long histories of civilisation, and the many centuries of the Silk Roads' operation saw goods traded in both directions, as well as a steady movement of peoples travelling for political, religious, commercial and military purposes. Thanks to the Silk Roads, diverse regions, countries and civilisations became connected throughout history. This made it possible for numerous countries and civilisations of different historical periods to adapt to, and to integrate with, various foreign cultural factors. In the process they became both stronger and more in open their views of the world – while at the same time inheriting and developing their own traditional cultures.

The present exhibition, *Longquan of the World: Longquan Celadon and Globalization,* is jointly organised by the Palace Museum, the Zhejiang Provincial Museum, and the Lishui Municipal People's Government of Zhejiang. It reflects the research accomplishments from a Compass Project of 2012-2014, supported by the China's State Administration of Cultural Heritage and entitled *Spreading of Ancient Chinese Ceramic Technology to Other Countries and Its Impact.* However, the exhibition extends well beyond this research project. On the basis of the ceramic technology and culture, represented by Longquan celadon ware itself, it aims to examine the wide distribution of Longquan celadon across the Old World during the 12-15th centuries before the new trade routes were discovered. In the process it also aims to understand the influences that Longquan celadon wares exerted on the ceramic technologies of various regions beyond China. While countries such as Vietnam, Thailand, Japan and Britain were able to fully copy Longquan celadon ware, other countries like Burma, Iran, Syria and Egypt applied their traditional ceramic technologies to recreate Longquan wares for local consumption. Although these reproductions varied between regions, they all resulted in local improvements in ceramic technology as a result of the communication and the merging of cultures through the Silk Roads. In this regard, Longquan celadon is of international significance. The worldwide appreciation and recreation of Longquan celadon may be seen as a driving force for globalization in these early years.

We extend our thanks to the Forbidden City Cultural Heritage Conservation Foundation, the Longfor Group, the Zhejiang Provincial Museum, and the Lishui Municipal People's Government of Zhejiang for great support to the exhibition. The valuable support and help from over forty museums, archaeological organisations, institutes and universities in China and other countries is appreciated. We also thank Mr. Geng Baochang and many colleagues at the Palace Museum for their tremendous efforts.

Wang Xudong
Director, the Palace Museum

序二

龙泉窑是宋元时期著名的青瓷窑口，因中心窑场位于浙南龙泉境内而得名。它创烧于晚唐五代，发展于北宋。宋室南渡后，更是融合了南北两大瓷业技艺，关联“官窑”“民窑”两个层次，集历代青瓷工艺之大成，成为中国古代陶瓷史上内涵丰富、产地广阔、规模壮观的青瓷窑业体系。

12 ~ 15 世纪，造型古朴端庄、釉质温润如玉的龙泉青瓷，畅销于亚洲、非洲和欧洲等地，成为该时期流布最广、产地最多的瓷器品类。其对世界陶瓷发展史影响最大，促进了跨区域技术、经济和文化的交流，为早期经济全球化奠定了基础。

近年来，大量的龙泉青瓷在国外被发现，有力地佐证了龙泉青瓷对外输出的历史记载，引起了学界的广泛关注。2010 年，我馆研究人员以“浙江青瓷在海外”为题开展专项调查与研究。2012 ~ 2014 年，我馆与故宫博物院等单位合作承担了国家文物局指南针计划——“中国古代瓷器生产技术对外传播研究”课题，探讨瓷器和制瓷技术在中国对外交流中的媒介作用和深远影响，并推出系列展览与国际学术活动。

多年来，承蒙故宫博物院的支持与帮助，两馆之间的交流与合作不断深入。此次，立足于两馆的藏品资源，特别是故宫博物院龙泉青瓷的藏品优势，同时汇集海内外数十家文博机构的数百件藏品，共襄盛举，联合举办“天下龙泉——龙泉青瓷与全球化”展览，旨在向公众展示龙泉青瓷在国内外广泛分布的时空面貌，并揭示其承载的深厚文化内涵和广泛的社会影响。

自古以来，文明的交流、互鉴，是推动人类社会进步和世界和平发展的重要动力。文明因交流而多彩，因互鉴而进步。瓷器的输出和文化的互动，筑就了连接世界的“陶瓷之路”，带动了中外贸易的发展，促进了东西方技艺的交流，丰富了沿线人民的物质和文化生活。其广博的历史文化内涵，对当今世界共建“一带一路”，具有深远的历史意义。

值此浙江省博物馆建馆九十周年之际，我馆联合故宫博物院、丽水市人民政府共同推出“天下龙泉——龙泉青瓷与全球化”展览及国际学术研讨会，是对自己生日的一份很好的纪念。

浙江省博物馆馆长 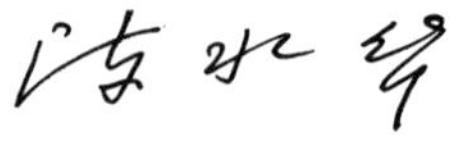

Preface II

The Longquan kilns are famous for their celadon production during the Song (960–1279) and Yuan (1279–1368) dynasties. They derive their name from the location of their primary kilns in Longquan, in south Zhejiang province. The manufacture of Longquan celadon started from late Tang dynasty (618-907) to the Five Dynasties (907–960) period and developed in the Northern Song dynasty (960–1127). During the Southern Song dynasty (1127–1279), the Longquan potters merged ceramic technologies of south and north China, integrated two levels of production, at imperial kilns and private kilns, and successfully incorporated technologies of green-glazed ceramics of successive dynasties. The Longquan kilns consequently became a celadon kiln system with a rich technology and a major cultural significance. They also combined wide regions of manufacture with the most magnificent scale of production in Chinese ceramic history.

During the Song and Yuan periods, Longquan wares featured archaistic and elegant forms and lustrous jade-like celadon glazes. They were widely exported to many parts of Asia, Africa and Europe. Longquan celadon became the ceramic type of this period that boasted of the widest geographical distribution, the largest number of places of manufacture, and the most profound influence upon the development of ceramic history in lands beyond China itself. By these means they boosted technology, and economic and cultural exchanges between different regions of the world, which laid a foundation for globalization in these early years.

The Zhejiang Provincial Museum has experienced increasingly deep exchanges and collaborations with the Palace Museum, thanks to its support and its help over many years. The present exhibition benefits from the strong collections of the two museums, in particular the outstanding Longquan celadons from the Ming and Qing (1368-1911) royal collections of the Palace Museum. With hundreds of objects kindly loaned from tens of other museums and cultural organisations in China and overseas, the Palace Museum and the Zhejiang Provincial Museum are able to present this magnificent exhibition, *Longquan of the World: Longquan Celadon and Globalization*. Our goal is to demonstrate to the public the wide distribution of Longquan celadon in and outside China over an extended period of history, and the deep and rich cultural significance and broad social influences embodied in these objects.

Throughout history, exchanges and mutual learning between different civilisations have been an important driving force for human progress and for global peace and development. Civilisations have become richer, more colourful and better developed through exchange and mutual learning. The exporting of ceramics and the interactions of cultures gave rise to the Ceramic Roads that made the world increasingly connected. This boosted the development of trade between China and other countries, promoted technological exchanges between the East and the West, and enriched materials and cultures for peoples along the Ceramic Roads. The broad historic and cultural significance of Chinese ceramics has profound implications for both the Silk Road Economic Belt and the 21st Century Maritime Silk Road that China and the world are currently building together.

On the 90th anniversary of the Zhejiang Provincial Museum, we present the exhibition *Longquan of the World: Longquan Celadon and Globalization* in Beijing and Hangzhou in collaboration with the Palace Museum and the Lishui Municipal People's Government. We will also collaborate with the Longquan Municipal People's Government to organise an international symposium in Longquan on the same subject. This is a good commemoration of the birthday of the Museum.

Chen Shuihua
Director, the Zhejiang Provincial Museum

序三

瓷器是中华文明孕育的伟大历史瑰宝、中华民族的劳动智慧结晶，是中国对人类文明、世界文化作出的重大贡献。绚丽夺目的瓷器桂冠上，龙泉青瓷以“青如玉、明如镜、声如磬”的特质惊艳天下，成为镶嵌桂冠上的璀璨明珠。

丽水地区早在两晋时期已经开始烧造瓷器，龙泉烧造青瓷起始于晚唐五代，宋代之后进入鼎盛，历经千余年兴盛不衰，更在古老的“丝绸之路”上演绎播撒了悠远中华文化的浪漫旋律，被欧洲人亲切地称为“雪拉同”。2009 年 9 月，龙泉青瓷传统烧制技艺作为全球唯一陶瓷类项目，被联合国教科文组织列入《人类非物质文化遗产代表作名录》，标志着龙泉青瓷与其背后蕴含的工匠精神成为全人类的共同精神和文化财富。

龙泉所处的丽水市，有着冠绝全国的生态优势，处处蕴含云淡天高的青瓷意境；有着巍峨绵延的江浙高峰，群山深藏丰富优质的瓷土资源；有着奔流入海的烟波瓯江，碧波漾起联通世界的开放虹桥；有着钟灵毓秀的深厚文化，滋养孕育万千变化的瓷制新意；有着崇耕尚读的淳朴乡土，世代造就厚德笃行的能工巧匠。

文明因交流互鉴而绚丽多彩。作为青瓷故乡的丽水市，此次与故宫博物院、浙江省博物馆合作，共同举办“天下龙泉——龙泉青瓷与全球化”展览，向世界展示龙泉青瓷发展历程，展现龙泉青瓷艺术之美，重现“丝绸之路”青瓷盛景，旨在通过交流互鉴弘扬青瓷文化，精进青瓷技艺，壮大青瓷产业，在守正创新中推动龙泉青瓷“深化、物化、转化”发展，让瓷器这个鲜明独特的中华文化标符焕发出更加璀璨夺目的时代光芒！

中共丽水市委书记　胡海峰

Preface Ⅲ

Porcelain is a great and historic invention and treasure of Chinese civilisation. As an outstanding example of the industriousness and wisdom of the Chinese nation, porcelain represents a significant Chinese contribution to both human civilization and to world culture. Longquan celadon is celebrated for being "green like jade, bright like a mirror, and with a sound like a chime stone". It is fascinating to the world, like a luminous jewel radiating on the brilliant crown of Chinese ceramics.

Ceramics were fired at the Tantou kiln site, Lishui as early as the Jin dynasty (266–420), while Longquan started to fire celadon from late Tang dynasty (618-907) to the Five Dynasties (907–960). From the Song dynasty (960–1279) onwards, production of celadon thrived in Longquan and lasted there for about a millennium. Longquan celadon was widely distributed along the Silk Roads, and, by these means, spread the beauty and romance of China's time-honoured culture. In Europe, the beautiful fashionable green-glazed wares from China is fondly called celadon, a name that derives from a French stage play of the 17th century, in which a shepherd boy called Celadon wore ribbons on his sleeves that were misty green and like the attractive colour of Longquan wares. In September 2009, UNESCO recognised and included the traditional firing technology of Longquan celadon on its Representative List of the Intangible Cultural Heritage of Humanity, which was the only ceramic technology listed. This signifies that Longquan celadon and the craftspeople's spirit that it embodies has become part of the common spiritual and cultural wealth shared by the whole of humankind.

Longquan is located in the Lishui region of Zhejiang, which respectively means 'Dragon Spring' and 'Beautiful Water/River'. The Lishui region boasts pristine ecological features unmatched in China, with bright sky and clean waters everywhere that are reminiscent of the charming Longquan celadon glaze. Lofty mountains and hills abound in Lishui and the region is rich in ceramic materials including high-grade clays. The Ou river runs towards the ocean where ports and green waves link Lishui to the world like a rainbow bridge. Well-endowed by nature, the Lishui region has long nurtured people of talent, and the rich culture of Lishui's long history has seen major innovations in its ceramic technology. The pure hearted and trustworthy country folk in Lishui highly value both industrious farming and enlightened reading, which gave rise to many generations of master artisans with outstanding virtues and skills.

Civilisations have become richer and more colourful through the processes of exchange and mutual learning. As the hometown of Longquan celadon, Lishui appropriately collaborates with the Palace Museum and the Zhejiang Provincial Museum to jointly organise the exhibition *Longquan of the World: Longquan Celadon and Globalization*. We aim to introduce the development trajectory of Longquan celadon and its charming beauty to the world, and present the historic vision of Longquan celadon blooming along the Silk Roads. We hope that exchanges and mutual learning of peoples and civilisations will help to promote celadon culture, improve celadon technology, and strengthen the celadon industry. Through the right means of perseverance, pragmatism and innovation, we wish that Longquan celadon will enter not only the ears but also the hearts of many people in China and overseas. We will provide solid industrial infrastructures for Longquan celadon culture, and facilitate its transcendence and transformation into a robust and sustainable economic pattern and system. Porcelain, a distinct hallmark of Chinese culture, shall shine still more brilliantly in the world of a new era!

Hu Haifeng
Secretary of Lishui Municipal Committee of the CPC , Zhejiang

天下龙泉

——龙泉青瓷与全球化

王光尧　故宫博物院
沈琼华　浙江省博物馆

《诗经·小雅·北山》有载“溥天之下，莫非王土；率土之滨，莫非王臣”，其“溥天之下”在自然指苍穹之下；在人文则指所有人类活动的地方。我们提出“天下龙泉”的概念[1]并用为展览的名称，就是依据中国古代的语境及古人关于世界的认识：中国古代所说的天下意即全世界，也就是今天所说的全球。宋元至明早中期的中国龙泉青瓷，不仅在中国有极高的认知度，而且输出到亚、非、欧三洲的许多国家，可以说是当时人类商贸、文化交流所及的全部世界，自然具有全球化的意义。本展览和本文所说的“天下龙泉”就是要叙述12～15世纪龙泉青瓷在中国本土的生产、发展和使用情况，龙泉青瓷在全世界的流布和使用情况，不同国家和地区对龙泉青瓷的使用、接受程度及这一事实产生的深远影响，以及由此表现出的龙泉青瓷的全球化情况。

一　何以龙泉

龙泉青瓷是后起且不断演进的概念，指宋、元、明时浙江省龙泉县（今龙泉市，下同）以大窑为中心的地区烧造的青瓷器，也包括同一个时期风格相同的青瓷器。

龙泉（县）窑的概念在南宋叶寘《坦斋笔衡》中已经存在，但统观文中叙述北宋末年受命为宫廷烧造青窑器之事，是把江南的龙泉县窑和“河北”的唐州、邓州、耀州、汝州四州的窑并列[2]，这里有可能只是一个官府管理机构的概念，有些宋代地方官窑的性质。

此后的元代到明代早期，龙泉青瓷被称为青窑器、青瓷器[3]、处器、青处器[4]、青器、土青器[5]、豆青瓷[6]。嘉靖十五年《七修类稿续稿》开始有“龙泉窑”“龙泉”的名称，且专指龙泉烧造的弟窑类瓷，明确指出之所以命名为“龙泉（或龙泉窑）”的原因是“以地名也”，同时也有以烧窑人的姓氏称之为章窑者[7]。自此，龙泉窑和龙泉瓷的名字开始流行。清乾隆《龙泉县志》仍然称为青瓷[8]，但在同一时期的清代宫廷文献中，如乾隆二十年（1755年）御制《咏龙泉盘子》诗记载新疆吐鲁番出土龙泉窑盘子时，明确使用了“龙泉盘子”“龙泉釉”“宋龙泉窑”的概念[9]，之后乾隆皇帝还写过《咏龙泉窑碗》《咏宋龙泉无当尊》诗[10]。文献表明，从明代晚期到清中期，从浙江地方到清代宫廷，在对传世或出土实物的认定中依据产地为归属原则，龙泉窑、龙泉瓷或龙泉釉已经成为一种共识，成为宋、元、明时期龙泉窑场产品的统称。

既然通过上文我们论证了什么是龙泉窑或龙泉青瓷，那么就要强调一点，即龙泉青瓷内涵的性质：谈龙泉地区的瓷器生产史，当然可以从唐代甚至更早的时间谈起，但是论龙泉青瓷或龙泉窑的生产历史，却断不可与该地区的瓷器生产史混为一谈。

从考古发掘资料可知，龙泉地区烧造青瓷器至迟在唐代已成规模，直到五代、北宋早期，当地的产品仍然有浓重的越窑、婺州窑的风格，部分产品甚至还受瓯窑的影响，该地区的窑场可视为越窑、婺州窑的地方性窑场。到北宋中期或更晚，在当地传统的灰青釉基础上，受北方耀州窑和定窑系刻花、划花及印花工艺影响，龙泉地区的窑场开始烧造单面刻花、双面刻划花或刻划花加篦点纹的瓷器，并逐渐形成龙泉地区青瓷产品的独特风格，由于这种风格的瓷器一直被认为是在龙泉地区的窑场首先烧成[11]，所以称这类风格的瓷器为龙泉青瓷，并把它们从越窑系中区分开来。龙泉地区窑场产品自我风格的形成，正值传统越窑风格衰落之时，原因虽值得深入研究，但龙泉窑继越窑之后成为浙江地区乃至整个中国青瓷的代表则是不争的事实。约当龙泉地区的青瓷产品发生上述风格的转变的同时，江西景德镇和金溪窑场等地的青白瓷、福建部分青瓷窑场产品，也与龙泉青瓷一样开始采用划花、篦点纹装饰，在装饰方法和装饰风格上都明显受到北方定窑瓷器工艺和装饰风格的影响。江西、浙江和福建如此大面积出现瓷器装饰相同、变化时间近同的现象，是中国陶瓷史上一个非常值得重视并深入研究的课题。

正是由于龙泉窑场在北宋晚期已成为浙江地区青瓷生产的代表，所以到北宋末年徽宗因定窑白瓷有芒，改命当时几处著名窑场烧造青窑器时，龙泉窑已在受命之列。龙泉青瓷由此开始和宫廷有了直接的关系，从民间走向庙堂。官府的直接介入，使得龙泉窑场进入了一个全新的时代。

二　成为时尚

《坦斋笔衡》:“江南则处州龙泉县窑。”《鸡肋编》:“处州龙泉县……又出青瓷器，谓之‘秘色’，钱氏所贡，盖取于此。宣和中，禁庭制样须索，益加工巧。”可以知道龙泉窑在北宋末年根据宫廷下发的官样为宫廷或官府烧造瓷器之事可资凭信[12]。距龙泉千里之外的宫廷下令其按宫廷颁发的样子烧造瓷器，此时大江以南为皇宫烧造瓷器的只有龙泉一处窑场，其地位在江南可想而知。

从对临安城的考古资料看，在已经发掘的几处南宋宫廷遗址内，出土瓷器标本中占比最多的都是龙泉青瓷，说明在南宋时期龙泉青瓷已经成为宫廷用瓷的主流，龙泉也成为宫廷用瓷的最大供应地。在南宋六陵遗址也出土了白胎龙泉窑瓷器，这又从另一个角度证明龙泉窑瓷器进入了南宋皇宫内。同样，考古资料表明，在南宋时期港口、都市、乡镇和一般墓葬出土瓷器中有大量的龙泉窑瓷器，可见龙泉窑瓷器在当时的社会生活中已经拥有一定的地位。

元朝统一，为龙泉青瓷在中国北方市场流行提供了机遇，龙泉青瓷真正开始占据包括今天蒙古在内的全国市场。对元大都、哈拉和林和阿力麻里的考古发掘表明，从帝国的都城到汗国王庭都大量使用龙泉青瓷。而在集宁路一级的地方性城镇和主要交通线上，也出土有大量龙泉青瓷，这成为元代龙泉青瓷通行全国的考古证据。

元代实行匠籍制，从元初几次大规模在浙西搜括匠人的情况看，大量无技艺者尚在其中，身怀窑业技术的龙泉窑瓷器匠人也必然会被搜括为官匠，制瓷匠人成为官府拥有的生产资料并从事生产，故而这一时期应该有大量隶属官府的龙泉窑场存在。史料中也有了龙泉窑为皇宫烧造瓷器的记载[13]。又据典志，元代祭祀参用国礼（即蒙古旧俗），牲首用马首，并承以盘，如果这种盘也是瓷盘的话，则清宫旧藏龙泉窑瓷器中的大盘就属于这种放置马首的礼祭器了。

明代是龙泉窑生产史上与皇宫关系最密切的时期，处州（今浙江省丽水市）从洪武时期就开始承担为皇宫烧造瓷器的任务。《大明会典》载：“洪武二十六年定，凡烧造供用器皿等物，须定夺样制，计算人工物料。如果数多，起取人匠赴京，置窑兴工。或数少，行移饶、处等府烧造。”[14]据此，不管所需瓷器数量多少，处州都承担了一定的生产任务。所以，不仅南京故宫遗址出土了大量的明初龙泉青瓷，而且在故宫博物院收藏的清宫旧藏瓷器中也有大量的明代龙泉青瓷。和宋元时期相比，清宫旧藏的明龙泉窑瓷器中，日用器的比例已大大增加，说明处州窑的产品除了充当礼祭器外，已成为皇宫日常用器具的重要来源。《明宪宗实录》天顺八年正月乙亥条记载：“江西饶州府、浙江处州府，见差内官在彼烧造瓷器，诏书到日，除已烧完者照数起解，未完者悉皆停止。差委官员，即便回京，违者罪之。”说明至少到天顺时期，一直都有从北京派来的太监在处州督陶，而且产品大量进入明宫廷的龙泉窑场绝不只是偶尔承担了生产宫廷用瓷的任务，应该与景德镇一样有专门为皇室生产瓷器的御窑存在。

除服务宫廷外，龙泉窑场的产品在明代早期是政府外交用瓷的最主要品种，这不仅可以从琉球王国各遗址出土瓷器中得到证明，在郑和下西洋的礼品中也有大量的龙泉青瓷。和龙泉枫洞岩窑址出土明代早期官式龙泉青瓷同样类型、品质的瓷器，在印度、阿拉伯联合酋长国、伊朗乃至肯尼亚等处的考古遗址中都有发现，这些遗址勾连成的航线正是郑和船队所到达的地方，亦见于中国文献记载或当地的传说。

不只宫廷，明代上层社会也流行使用龙泉青瓷，徐达、宋晟、俞通海等明代功臣墓或家族墓地成组（套）出土龙泉青瓷，不仅显示了当时龙泉青瓷的地位，也成为研究明代早期龙泉青瓷使用情况的重要资料，乃至是研究从宋元社会向明代转变过程中龙泉青瓷造型变化与器用组合方式的第一手资料。

三　走向海外

龙泉青瓷在中国域内已然如此，在中国以外也同样深得各个阶层人士的喜爱。从国内外考古资料所见，南宋时期的龙泉青瓷已经成为当时中国最主要的外贸商品，从东亚到东南亚、南亚、西亚再到非洲东部和北部，在古代的传统贸易区域内到处都可以看到龙泉青瓷的身影。

宋室南迁，为增加财政收入，发展贸易成为国家支持的行为，商业需求使得此时龙泉窑生产达到高峰期。龙泉青瓷不仅行销江南各地，也大量销往海外，而且以日用类的碗、盘为最大宗产品。仅经考古发掘的印度奎隆港口遗址、阿拉伯联合酋长国祖尔法遗址、伊朗霍尔木兹古城遗址、肯尼亚拉姆群岛和曼布鲁伊河口遗址、埃及福斯塔特遗址和英国威廉姆森在波斯湾沿岸调查过的数十处遗址等处，都有南宋、元、明早期的龙泉青瓷出土。这些不仅说明龙泉青瓷是从南宋到元明早期数百年间中国的主要出口商品，而且足以证明当时的中外文化交流和贸易繁荣的程度，是当今构建、复原海上丝绸之路不可或缺的实物证据。

元朝统一后，沿袭宋朝鼓励外贸的经济政策，甚至采用官本船的方式支持对外贸易。在当时的对外贸易产值比中，瓷器是仅次于丝绸的大宗外销商品，在东亚、南亚、西亚、东非等主要遗址出土的中国元代瓷器中，龙泉窑瓷器均占有相当的比重。大约也在同一时期，龙泉青瓷进入金帐汗国统治下的东欧。根据法国考古出土的一些龙泉青瓷碎片，可以知道龙泉青瓷约在同一个时期进入法国[15]，初识龙泉青瓷的法国人惊叹龙泉青色之美，赠送龙泉青瓷一个诗化的名字——Celadon，至今该名称仍是西方语言对龙泉青瓷和青瓷的通用名。

图1　龙泉窑青釉刻划花卉纹盘残件
印度 Purana Qila 皇宫遗址出土

图2　龙泉窑青釉器残件
越南河内京城考古研究所藏

图3　龙泉窑青釉刻缠枝莲纹凤尾尊
日本冲绳考古所藏

图 4　越南仿龙泉青釉刻莲瓣纹碗残件
越南河内京城考古研究所藏

图 5　泰国仿龙泉青釉刻变形莲瓣纹罐
故宫博物院藏

同时，龙泉青瓷不仅是波斯伊儿汗国皇宫内的明珠，在稍后的萨法维王朝，来自中国的龙泉青瓷和元青花瓷器被刻上铭记后供奉在阿德比尔陵的神殿内。当奥斯曼土耳其帝国在与伊朗萨法维王朝的战争中取得胜利后，即把包括大量龙泉青瓷在内的中国瓷器作为战利品运回伊斯坦布尔。或许这些瓷器原本就是奥斯曼土耳其觊觎的对象。除伊儿汗国、金帐汗国外，察合台汗国都城所在地霍城县阿力麻里从清代以来一直有龙泉青瓷出土，在伊拉克巴格达宫殿遗址、印度莫卧儿王朝的皇宫内也出土了龙泉青瓷（图1），在安南（今越南北部）升龙府皇宫遗址（图2）、琉球各王国的几处王国宫殿遗址同样也有大量的元明时期的龙泉青瓷出土（图3）。远在东非的肯尼亚海滨各主要宫殿遗址所见元明早期的中国瓷器更是以龙泉青瓷占据主导地位，北非的福斯塔特（开罗旧城）出土瓷器中龙泉青瓷也占有相当的比例。上述资料显示，从沿海到内地，从乡村到都市，从民居到皇宫，龙泉青瓷成为当时世界的时尚。另据中国文献记载，当时到中国朝贡的琉球使臣还违禁到龙泉自行购买青瓷，可见他们对龙泉青瓷的渴求程度[16]。

一直以来，龙泉青瓷深受日本人的喜爱，迄今见诸日本公私收藏的龙泉青瓷中不乏被定为国宝或重要文化财者。它们大多是在南宋、元时期作为商品进入日本的，和这些在日本传世的龙泉青瓷相比，韩国新安沉船等沉没船只是其中的一个不幸。明永乐时期，日本使臣曾奉将军之命携带一枚碗口有破冲的南宋龙泉青瓷碗来明，因为将军太过钟爱，请求明廷再赐一枚同样的碗。但是，从南宋到明初，龙泉青瓷的风格已经发生了很大的变化，不管是明朝君臣、还是来华使臣，都无法搜罗到同样的龙泉青瓷碗，所以只能请人锔补后再带回日本，孰料锔补后碗的青釉和深褐色的锔钉形成了完美的搭配，被日本称为“马蝗绊”，一时名重天下，传承至今。

四　普世之美

从南宋到明代早期即 12 世纪中期至 15 世纪中期，龙泉青瓷在当时全世界范围内的流行程度和时尚效应，在新航线开辟、新世界发现以前的东西方文化交流史上无出其右。也正是在这种广泛认同的基础上，中国输出的龙泉青瓷开始从单纯的商品输出转向更深层的文化与技术层面的输出。

我们曾经以瓷器为媒介讨论过中外文化交流的三个层次[17]：最初级的交流只局限于商品的流通，即输出和输入，以及对产品的简单了解；进一步的交流是通过对输入商品的了解，以本土的技术和原料模仿输出的商品；最高层次的交流是生产技术的直接交流，以及对输入商品的真正理解并实现和原产地一样的量化生产。反观龙泉青瓷走向全世界的历程，基本经历了上述三个层次的交流。尤其是越南、泰国、缅甸、伊朗、埃及、日本、英国、韩国等地，都曾仿烧过龙泉青瓷，这种仿烧既有如越南（图4）、泰国（图5）、日本（图6、图7）、英国在不同时期仿烧的真正高温青釉瓷，

图6　日本仿龙泉青釉印花盘
日本九州市立陶瓷文化馆藏

图7　日本仿龙泉青釉印山水图三足筒式炉
日本九州市立陶瓷文化馆藏

图8　伊朗仿龙泉青釉印四鱼纹折沿盘
英国维多利亚与艾伯特博物馆藏

也有其他各国用其本土的陶瓷胎釉技术进行的仿烧，产品的釉色、品质固然各不相同，但是归纳起来则表现为对龙泉青瓷器的釉色、造型（如折沿、菱花口）和纹饰（如双鱼纹、莲瓣纹）的模仿（图8），这种模仿的背后是当时从东亚到东南亚、西亚和非洲，以及后来的英国，对来自中国的龙泉青瓷及龙泉青瓷所代表的瓷器文化的认同。同时我们还观察到泰国、越南、缅甸、伊朗等国的仿龙泉窑产品，除了满足本国市场外，也向世界其他市场投放，这说明龙泉青瓷市场国际化的同时，它的产地也是国际性的。这是一种世界范围内表现在陶瓷器上的、通过文化交流实现先进文化全球化过程以及各地区的陶瓷文化相互融合、共同发展的实例。这种不同地区、不同国家对龙泉青瓷的认同和共同的文化追求，正是本文和本展览要表达的“天下龙泉”的含义。

结语

当前，不管是在中国还是在外国，谈到古代东西方不同文明中心间的文化交流，多采用丝绸之路、海上丝绸之路或陶瓷之路的名称，也有使用棉花之路、香料之路、宝石之路、朝圣之路等不同概念者，名称和概念虽异，但都是对古代不同部族、不同地区或国家之间的文化交流情况和文化交流通道史迹的表述。在这个交流的大道上，行进着为政治、宗教、商业、军事等不同目的的人群，甚至也有仅仅为谋求自身生存的人，往往都怀抱对未知世界的探求和对美好生活的向往与追求。正是在这一目标的促使下，数千年间，从东方到西方，从太平洋沿岸到大西洋之滨，在亚洲、欧洲、非洲之间的文化交流和产品交流的行程一直不曾中断。12 ~ 15 世纪，中国龙泉青瓷的输出和在世界各地的流行，在给各地人民带来美好物质文明享受的同时，也以先进的瓷器生产技术和瓷器文化促进了各地陶瓷生产技术的提高，并形成长达 300 余年世界范围内的一个文化认同。不同地区、不同国家在相互之间商品流动的基础上，促成了相互交流、学习，并带来生产技术的普遍提高，正是丝绸之路的历史真相与价值所在（本文曾发表于《故宫博物院院刊》2019 年第 7 期，本书略有改动）。

注释

1 本文所说的“天下龙泉”，与故宫博物院、浙江省博物馆和丽水市人民政府联合举办的“天下龙泉——龙泉青瓷与全球化”展览的概念一样，有一个发展的过程。首先是在2012年浙江省博物馆举办“大元帆影”展时，王光尧与沈琼华商量想联合举办一个关于龙泉青瓷的更大的展览，并称为“天下龙泉”，但是当时的想法只是中国龙泉产品在世界各国流布情况，并没有包括各国仿龙泉瓷器及其代表的文化认同、共同标准等内容，也就是说当时关于龙泉青瓷的认识仍局限在中国传统的范畴内。到2013年1月，沈琼华、王光尧、小林仁、森达也四人在琉球考察当地出土的中国龙泉窑瓷器，又在九州观摩日本仿龙泉青瓷时首议今天本文所说的“天下龙泉”的概念，在中国龙泉青瓷外，已包括外国仿龙泉青瓷产品。2013年12月至2014年1月，王光尧、沈琼华、沈岳明、森达也四人在越南考察瓷窑址时惊诧于越南仿龙泉的水平之高，商定使用并推出“天下龙泉”概念。浙江省博物馆把“天下龙泉”课题和同名展览确定为2015年的项目。其后，王光尧于2016年在“越瓷文化学术研讨会”详细阐述了天下龙泉的概念（说见《越地精粹 青瓷宏篇——浙江青瓷与官府的关系及其在世界瓷器史上的地位》，《越瓷文化学术研讨会论文集》，中国文联出版社，2018年）；沈岳明发表《河滨遗范　天下龙泉》（《世界遗产》2016年第6期）；浙江省博物馆于2018年1月举办“太仓樊村泾遗址出土文物展暨天下龙泉·2018’学术研讨会”。

2 值得说明的是，《坦斋笔衡》中关于“江南则处州龙泉县窑”和“河北唐、邓、耀州悉有之，汝窑为魁”的概念，根据常识性的地理知识可知，处州龙泉县在江南不误，而唐州、邓州、耀州、汝州四地没有一处在黄河以北（即一般性认知的河北）。那么，《坦斋笔衡》代表的南宋知识层为何称唐州、邓州、耀州、汝州四地为“河北”？这颇费解，此或许与南宋对金称臣，并割淮河大散关以北唐、邓二州给金有关，对南宋士子来说已是极大的耻辱，对割地之事自然更是讳言，“河北”或许是当时对割金之地的代称。同样，在南宋文献中使用“北地”或许也有此意。“北地郑州”“柴窑出北地”等记载详见《百宝总珍集》《格古要论》等书，不一一注出。《坦斋笔衡》见元陶宗仪《南村辍耕录》卷二十九“窑器”条引：“本朝以定州白磁器有芒不堪用，遂命汝州造青窑器。故河北唐、邓、耀州悉有之，汝窑为魁；江南则处州龙泉县窑，质颇粗厚。政和间，京师自置窑烧造，名曰官窑。中兴渡江，有邵成章提举后苑，号邵局，袭故京遗制，置窑于修内司，造青器，名内窑。澄泥为范，极其精致，油色莹彻，为世所珍。后郊坛下别立新窑，比旧窑大不侔矣。”中华书局，1959年。

3 （宋）庄绰：《鸡肋编》卷上：“处州龙泉县多佳树，地名豫章……又出青瓷器，谓之‘秘色’，钱氏所贡，盖取于此。宣和中，禁庭制样须索，益加工巧。”

4 （元）汪大渊：《岛夷志略》卷一“花面”：“地产牛、羊、鸡、鸭、槟郎、甘蔗、老叶、木棉，货用铁条、青布、粗碗、青处器之属。”文渊阁四库全书本。

5 （明）申时行等：《大明会典》卷三十五户部二十二“课程四·商税”：“凡税收……（洪武二十三年）又令各处税课司局商税，俱三十分税一，不得多收……景泰二年，令大兴、宛平二县……其收税则例：……青大碗每二十五个，青中碗每三十个，青大碟每十五个，税钞、牙钱钞、塌房钞各七百四十文……酒坛、土酒海每个，青中碟每五十个，白大盘每十个……税钞、牙钱钞、塌房钞各六百七十文；青小碟每五十个，白中盘每十五个，税钞、牙钱钞、塌房钞各六百文……青大盘每十二个，青盘每十五个，青小盘每二十个，青小碗每三十个……税钞、牙钱钞、塌房钞各五百文……土青盘每十五个，土青碗、小白盘每二十个，土青碟每五十个，青茶盅每七个，税钞、牙钱钞、塌房钞各四百文……土青酒盅、土青茶盅每十二个，土青香炉、大白碗每十个，中白碗每十五个，白大碟每二十个，白小碟每二十五个，税钞、牙钱钞、塌房钞各三百文……白小碗每十五个，税钞、牙钱钞、塌房钞各二百文。”第255～256页。

6 （明）申时行等：《大明会典》卷一百一十三礼部七十一“给赐番夷通例”：“凡折还物价，弘治间定……青花白瓷盘每个五百贯，碗每个三百贯，瓶每个五百贯，酒海每个一千五百贯；豆青瓷盘每个一百五十贯、碗每个一百贯，瓶每个一百五十贯。”第599页。

7 （明）郎瑛：《七修类稿续编》卷六“七修续稿事物类·二窑”条：“哥窑与龙泉窑皆出处州龙泉县。南宋时有章生一、生二兄弟，各主一窑，生一所陶者为哥窑，以兄故也；生二所陶者为龙泉，以地名也。其色皆青，浓淡不一，其足皆铁色，亦浓淡不一，旧闻紫足，今少见焉。惟土脉细薄，油水纯粹者最贵。哥窑则多断文，号百圾破，龙泉窑至今温、处人称为章窑。”清乾隆耕烟草堂本。

8 《龙泉县志》卷三“赋役志·青瓷窑”：“青瓷窑（一都琉田）……化治以后，质粗色恶，难充雅玩矣。”清乾隆二十七年修，同治二年补刊本，“中国方志丛书”第六〇六号，台北成文出版有限公司，1984年。

9 《清高宗（乾隆）御制诗文全集》第三集卷九十二“咏龙泉盘子”，第五册第739页，中国人民大学出版社，2013年。

10 《清高宗（乾隆）御制诗文全集》第四集卷十四“咏龙泉窑碗”、第四集卷四十二“咏宋龙泉无当尊”，第六册第452页、962页，中国人民大学出版社，2013年。

11 在黄岩沙埠窑发现之后，关于这种双面刻划花加篦点纹的瓷器是否是在龙泉地区首烧，有值得进一步研究的必要，但这类瓷器是北方制瓷工艺影响浙江地区青瓷生产的结果则可以肯定。

12 王光尧：《关于清宫旧藏龙泉窑瓷器的思考——官府视野下的龙泉窑》，浙江省考古研究所等编《大窑枫洞岩窑址出土瓷器》，文物出版社，2009年；沈琼华：《龙泉窑与官府和宫廷的关系》，2012年在日本爱知县陶瓷资料馆演讲稿。

13 《元史》卷七十四“祭祀三”记载：“中统以来，杂金宋祭器而用之。至治初，始造新器于江浙行省，其旧器悉置几阁。”

14 （明）申时行等：《大明会典》卷一百九十四工部十四“窑冶 · 陶器”，明万历内府刻本。

15 有两片中国青瓷残片出土于法国阿维尼翁教皇宫西侧花园内，花园修建时间为 1365 ～ 1367 年。Dominique CARRU al., *De l'Orientà la table du Pape: L'importation des céramiquesdans la régiond'Avignon au MoyenÂgetardif (XIVe-XVIesiècles)* , Service d'archéologieVaucluse, 1995, p34. No.28.

16 《明太宗实录》记载：“（永乐二年五月）甲辰，礼部尚书李至刚等奏：‘琉球国山南王遣贡方物，就令赍白金诣处州市磁器，法当逮问。’上曰：‘远方之人知求利而已，安知禁令。朝廷于远人当怀之，此不足罪。’”另，《礼部志稿》卷二“怀远人之训”、卷九十二“不罪赍金市磁器”条所记同，《文渊阁四库全书》（597）第 42 页、《文渊阁四库全书》（598）第 658 页。《明史》卷三百二十三列传第二百一十一《琉球传》对此事也有记载。

17 王光尧：《以瓷器为媒介的中外文化交流层次》，浙江省博物馆编《2012 海上丝绸之路——中国古代瓷器输出及文化影响国际学术研讨会论文集》，浙江人民美术出版社，2013 年。

Longquan of the World: Longquan Celadon and Globalization

Wang Guangyao, the Palace Museum
Shen Qionghua, the Zhejiang Provincial Museum

We propose the concept of Tianxia Longquan (Longquan of the world) and we will use this as the main Chinese title for the present exhibition. Tianxia means Under Heaven and is a traditional Chinese term for an ancient Chinese cultural concept that denotes the entire geographical world. Longquan celadon wares, made in China during the Song (960-1279), Yuan (1279-1368) and early to middle Ming dynasty (1368–1644) are not only highly regarded across China, but were also exported to many countries in Asia, Africa and Europe. These regions represent the whole Old World that the commercial and cultural interactions of mankind had reached – representing the globalization of those early days.

The present exhibition and this essay aim to present various aspects of Longquan celadon during the 12-15th centuries: their production, development and use in China; their distribution to and use in the world; the variable uses and acceptance of Longquan celadon in different countries and regions, and the profound influences that they exerted, both at home and abroad. Taken together, these various aspects of Longquan celadon's history amount to the globalization of this remarkable commodity.

Longquan celadon is a term that originated at a late stage and then underwent evolution. It refers to ceramics with high-fired green glaze made in regions in and around Dayao of Longquan county (today's Longquan city) and nearby areas during the Song to Ming dynasties, as well as contemporary celadon with very similar styles to such products.

The concept of 'Longquan (county) wares' already existed in the Southern Song (1127-1279) work of *Tan zhai bi heng* (Considered writings from the altar study) by Ye Zhi. In this book, he lists the 'Longquan county kilns (i.e., wares)' of south China (Jiangnan) alongside four wares from north China, namely those from the prefectures of Ruzhou, Tangzhou, Dengzhou, and Yaozhou. In this context, Ye Zhi was perhaps only using the expression to refer to an official management agency in Longquan that may be a type of local official kiln.

At the end of the Northern Song dynasty (960–1127), the Longquan kilns fired celadon for the royal court and government, based on official patterns sent from the court. In the Southern Song period, celadon from the Longquan region had already become the primary ceramics used at the royal court, and Longquan became the largest supplier for court ceramics. Products from Longquan also played a remarkable role in contemporary urban life. During the Yuan dynasty, celadon from Longquan gradually reached the entre domestic market of China. The Ming dynasty saw the closest connection between the Longquan kilns and the royal court, and Longquan potters started to fire ceramics for the royal court as early as the reign of Hongwu (1368-1398), the founding emperor of Ming dynasty. Amongst the Ming dynasty Longquan products, collected by the court of the Qing dynasty (1644-1911), were increasing numbers of Longquan wares intended for everyday life.

The presence of a large amount of Longquan products at the Ming royal court implies that the Longquan kilns did not manufacture for the court on only an occasional basis. Instead, certain imperial kilns operated in Longquan in much the same way as those in Jingdezhen in Jiangxi province that produced exclusively for the royal court. In addition to those made for the court, products from Longquan were also the main type of ceramic used in diplomacy during the early Ming period.

In addition to China, Longquan celadons were also deeply appreciated by peoples of different walks of life in other countries. Worldwide archaeological discoveries demonstrate that Longquan celadon had already become the most important export goods during the Southern Song dynasty, and there are archaeological finds or local collections of Longquan celadon in all traditional trade regions of the Old World, from East Asia, Southeast Asia, South Asia, West Asia, to East Africa and North Africa.

Amongst Yuan dynasty ceramics excavated from major archaeological sites in East Asia, South Asia, West Asia and East Africa, Longquan products account for a very considerable ratio. During approximately the same period, Longquan celadon entered the regions of East Europe that were under the rule of the Kipchak Khanate (the Golden Horde or Ulus of Jochi, 1240s–1502). Some fragments of Longquan celadon excavated in France imply that they also entered France around this same period. Longquan celadon has also been much cherished in Japan for many centuries, and most pieces in Japan were brought there as a commodity during the Southern Song and Yuan dynasties. Longquan celadon became an important fashion of the world, appreciated from the coasts to inland regions, from the countryside to cities, and from commoners' residences to royal palaces.

The widespread distribution of Longquan celadon across the world during the 12-15th centuries brought material pleasure and enjoyment to the peoples of the receiving countries. Furthermore, the advanced ceramic technology and ceramic culture from China also served as a driving force for the improvement of local ceramic technology in various regions. A widespread appreciation of green-glazed ceramics represented by Longquan celadon formed and this lasted for some 300 years, with great international impact. Commodity exchanges between different regions and countries lead to communication and mutual learning – together with general improvements in certain technologies – and this is the historic truth and value of the Silk Roads.

图版目录

List of Plates

图版

Plates

浙江地区的龙泉青瓷

浙江省是中国古代青瓷的传统产地，从原始青瓷的烧造到龙泉青瓷的烧造，积淀了深厚的青瓷文化底蕴。龙泉地区烧造瓷器有一千多年历史，当地窑场在越窑、瓯窑风格的基础上，不断融合北方制瓷技术，至北宋早中期形成了自己独特的风格，其产品开始称为龙泉窑器。至明代中期，龙泉窑一直是中国青瓷生产的代表，其产品除供应民间及海外市场，还有一部分特殊器物成为宫廷用瓷的主要品种。明代中期以后，龙泉窑生产逐渐衰落。明代晚期，受景德镇青釉技术影响，龙泉青瓷产品风格有所改变，其在市场上和社会上的影响逐渐变弱。20 世纪 50 年代以后，借助现代自然科学技术，龙泉青瓷恢复烧造，龙泉窑从此步入现代化的生产时代。

The Celadon Wares of Longquan, Zhejiang

Zhejiang province is the traditional place for production of greenwares in Chinese history. From green-glazed proto-porcelain (*yuanshi qingci*) of thousands years ago to the firing of Longquan celadon, Zhejiang boasts of a rich and long history of greenware culture. The Longquan region in Zhejiang has a history of over a millennium for celadon production. Based on other ceramic traditions in Zhejiang including Yue ware and Ou ware, potters in Longquan also integrated ceramic techniques from north China. By the early and middle Northern Song dynasty, ceramics fired in Longquan formed its own unique style, and started to be known as "Longquan wares". Longquan celadon had remained as the representative for Chinese greenware until the middle Ming dynasty. In addition to domestic and overseas markets, some special objects fired in Longquan also became the primary vessels used by the Chinese court during certain periods. Starting in the middle Ming, the celadon production in Longquan gradually declined. The late Ming dynasty saw some changes in the style of Longquan celadon due to influence of celadon techniques from Jingdezhen, Jiangxi, and Longquan celadon gradually became less influential in market and society. With the help of modern scientific techniques, the 1950s saw a revival of celadon in Longquan, and the Longquan kilns entered the era of modern production.

001 龙泉窑青釉器残件（6件）

元

浙江省大窑

浙江省博物馆藏

元代龙泉窑采用的装饰技法丰富多样，其中以点彩和露胎技法最为新颖独特。露胎主要运用在制作精细的盘、碗类器物上，纹样丰富，有人物、动物等纹样，立体感强，具有浅浮雕的艺术效果。（江屿）

Fragments of Longquan celadon ware

Yuan dynasty, Dayao of Zhejiang Province,The Zhejiang Provincial Museum

002 龙泉窑青釉器残件（2件）

明早期
浙江省大窑
浙江省博物馆藏

明早期的龙泉青瓷，有一类器物制作工整、纹样精细、釉色滋润、器形庞大，其造型、纹饰与同时期景德镇御窑烧造的青花瓷器相同，应是专为宫廷烧造的器物。（江屿）

Fragments of Longquan celadon ware
Early Ming dynasty, Dayao of Zhejiang Province,The Zhejiang Provincial Museum

003 麻垟窑青釉器残件（8件）

元

浙江省博物馆藏

麻垟窑位于浙江省南部云和县，所产青瓷属龙泉东区窑场产品。宋代，龙泉青瓷的烧造以龙泉南区的金村、大窑、溪口为主。元代，为适应外销需求，龙泉东区也开始大规模生产青瓷，其产品在海外遗址常有出土。（江屿）

Fragments of Mayang kiln celadon ware

Yuan dynasty, The Zhejiang Provincial Museum

004 大山窑青釉器残件（7件）

元

浙江省博物馆藏

元代烧造龙泉青瓷风格产品的窑场分布地域广阔，浙江省温州市永嘉县境内出现了许多烧造龙泉青瓷风格产品的窑场，烧造的器物造型有碗、盘、高足杯、炉等。釉色豆青，色泽淡雅。装饰技法以印花为主，同时出现了模印文字。（江屿）

Fragments of Dashan kiln celadon ware

Yuan dynasty, The Zhejiang Provincial Museum

005 青釉刻划花卉纹折沿盘

明晚期

高 8.5 厘米　口径 39.5 厘米　足径 15 厘米

龙泉地区窑口

故宫博物院藏

盘敞口，圆唇，折沿，浅弧腹，圈足。内外通体施青釉，釉色翠青，釉面玻璃质感强，且遍布细碎开片。盘内底和内壁刻划折枝花纹。外底无釉，呈红褐色。足端裹釉。（蒋艺）

Celadon dish with everted rim and carved and incised floral design

Late Ming dynasty, Height 8.5cm mouth diameter 39.5cm foot diameter 15cm, Kiln of Longquan area, The Palace Museum

新113038

006 青釉刻划花卉纹折沿盘

明晚期

高 10.5 厘米　口径 45.5 厘米　足径 18.9 厘米

龙泉地区窑口

故宫博物院藏

盘敞口，厚唇，折沿，浅弧腹，圈足。通体内外施青釉，釉色翠青，釉面玻璃质感强，且遍布细碎开片纹。盘内底和内壁刻划折枝花卉纹。外底无釉，呈红褐色。胎体厚重，足端裹釉，可见多处垂釉和积釉。（蒋艺）

Celadon dish with everted rim and carved and incised floral design

Late Ming dynasty, Height 10.5cm mouth diameter 45.5cm foot diameter 18.9cm, Kiln of Longquan area, The Palace Museum

福建地区的仿龙泉青瓷

宋元时期，福建地区有许多窑场烧造青瓷，主要有松溪县西门窑和同安窑、福清市福清窑、莆田市庄边窑、漳浦县南门坑窑、罗源县八井村窑、东山县磁窑村窑等。福建地区生产的仿龙泉青瓷以外刻复线、内饰篦划纹者为多，与龙泉青瓷装饰风格相似，但产品质量和制作精细程度稍逊于龙泉青瓷。

Imitations of Longquan Celadon Fired in Fujian

Many areas in Fujian fired celadon during the Song and Yuan periods. These primarily include the Ximen kilns in Songxi county, the Tong'an kilns, the Fuqing kilns in Fuqing city, the Zhuangbian kilns in Putian city, the Nanmenkeng kilns in Zhangpu county, the Bajingcun kilns in Luoyuan county, the Ciyaocun (lit. 'porcelain kiln village') kilns in Dongshan county, etc. The Longquan style celadon fired in Fujian are primarily vessels with carved striations outside and combed design inside. Although looking similar to Longquan celadon in decorative style, the Fujian copies are inferior in terms of product quality and exquisite workmanship.

007 福清窑青釉器残件（4件）

宋

故宫博物院藏

福清窑位于福建省福清市，由多个窑场组成。烧造青釉产品的窑场有东张窑、石坑窑、岭下窑等。东张窑烧造的青釉碗多刻划篦点纹、外刻直线纹。石坑窑烧造的青釉碗、盘类器内常装饰篦划纹、篦点折线纹，外壁多刻成组的直线纹，足部修坯规整。岭下窑烧造的青釉篦划纹碗质量普遍较高。（王照宇）

Fragments of Fuqing kiln celadon ware

Song dynasty, The Palace Museum

008 福清窑青釉刻划缠枝花纹碗残件

宋

故宫博物院藏

碗施青釉，釉色青中泛黄，足端及足内无釉。碗内壁刻缠枝花纹，其间辅以“Z”字形走向的篦点纹，内底刻团菊纹。碗外壁斜刻条纹。（王照宇）

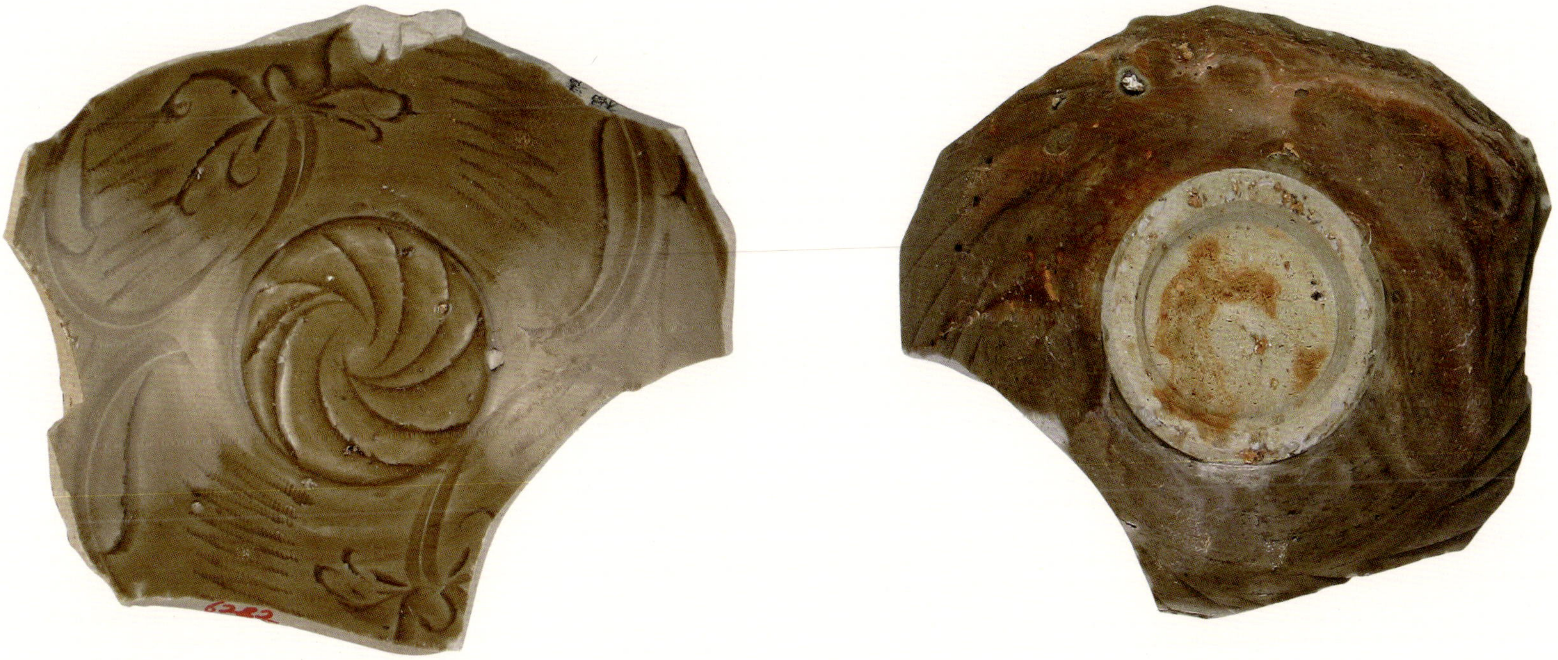

Fragment of Fuqing kiln celadon bowl with carved and incised floral scrolls design

Song dynasty, The Palace Museum

009 **同安窑青釉器残件**（3件）

宋

故宫博物院藏

同安窑位于福建省厦门市同安区，主要烧造青釉及青白釉两类瓷器。青釉釉色偏黄，碗类器里多以篦点、篦划纹装饰，外部刻划条纹。（王照宇）

Fragments of Tong'an kiln celadon ware

Song dynasty, The Palace Museum

010 同安窑青釉刻划花卉水波纹折腰盘残件

宋

故宫博物院藏

盘撇口，折腰，圈足。内、外施青釉，釉色青中泛黄，足端及足内无釉。内底刻划花卉纹，篦划水波纹。外壁刻数组条纹。（王照宇）

Fragment of Tong'an kiln celadon dish with angled wall and carved and incised design of floral and waves

Song dynasty, The Palace Museum

011 漳浦窑青釉器残件（6件）

宋

故宫博物院藏

漳浦窑位于福建省漳州市漳浦县，由南山窑、南门坑窑、竹树山窑和赤土窑等多个窑场组成，产品以青釉瓷为主，兼烧青白釉与黑褐釉瓷。器物造型常见碗、盘、壶等。装饰工艺以刻划花、印花为主。纹饰常见莲瓣纹、团菊纹、水波纹等。（王照宇）

Fragments of Zhangpu kiln celadon ware
Song dynasty, The Palace Museum

012 漳浦窑青釉刻划花卉篦点纹碗残件

宋

故宫博物院藏

碗敞口，弧腹，圈足。内、外施青釉，釉色青绿。施釉不及底，近足处、足端及足内无釉。碗内刻划花卉纹，并辅以篦点纹。碗外壁光素无纹饰。器身粘连残留的匣钵。（王照宇）

Fragment of Zhangpu kiln celadon bowl with carved and incised design of floral and spots

Song dynasty, The Palace Museum

013 八井村窑青釉器残件（4 件）

宋

故宫博物院藏

八井村窑位于福建省福州市罗源县八井村碗窑里，始烧于宋代，延续烧造时间较长。宋代产品主要有青釉瓷、青白釉瓷和黑釉瓷等，以青釉瓷为主，器物造型常见碗、盘、钵等。以内壁装饰篦划纹、外壁刻线纹为主。（王照宇）

Fragments of Bajingcun kiln celadon ware

Song dynasty, The Palace Museum

014 八井村窑青釉刻花纹碗残件

宋

故宫博物院藏

碗内、外施青釉，釉色青绿，积釉处玻璃质感较强。外壁施釉不及底，近足处、足端及足内无釉。碗内壁刻花卉纹。胎色灰黄。（王照宇）

Fragment of Bajingcun kiln celadon bowl with carved design

Song dynasty, The Palace Museum

015 东山窑青釉器残件（5件）

宋

故宫博物院藏

东山窑位于福建省漳州市东山县，由东山磁窑村窑、后壁山窑和后崂山等窑场组成。宋代始烧，产品以青釉瓷器为主。器物造型常见碗、盘、罐等。纹饰以刻划花卉纹、篦点折线纹、印花团菊纹为主。（王照宇）

Fragments of Dongshan kiln celadon ware

Song dynasty, The Palace Museum

016 东山窑青釉刻花篦点纹碗残件

宋

故宫博物院藏

碗内、外施青釉，釉色青中泛黄。外壁施釉不及底，有流釉现象。近足处、足端及足内无釉。碗内壁以刻划花卉纹装饰，其间辅以篦点纹。外壁斜刻条纹。（王照宇）

Fragment of Dongshan kiln celadon bowl carved with design of floral and spots

Song dynasty, The Palace Museum

017 莆田窑青釉器残件（4件）

宋

故宫博物院藏

莆田窑位于福建省莆田市，由庄边窑、碗林窑、碗里窑和五斗窑等多个窑场组成。产品以青釉瓷为主。器类常见碗、盘、瓶、罐、高足碗等。纹饰以刻划花卉纹或模印牡丹纹、莲花纹为主。（王照宇）

Fragments of Putian kiln celadon ware

Song dynasty, The Palace Museum

018 莆田窑青釉印双鱼纹折沿盘残件

南宋至元

故宫博物院藏

盘折沿，浅弧壁，圈足。内、外施青釉，釉色青绿，釉层较薄，釉层欠均匀。外壁施釉不及底，近足处、足端及足内无釉。盘内底有一涩圈无釉，系圈足叠烧处。盘内心印双鱼纹，鱼小巧可爱。（王照宇）

Fragment of Putian kiln celadon dish with everted rim and applied twin fish design

From Song dynasty to Yuan dynasty, The Palace Museum

019 石寨窑青釉碗残件

元

通高 8.5 厘米　口径 13.7 厘米　足径 5.3 厘米

福建博物院文物考古研究所藏

碗圆唇，撇口，深弧腹，圈足。灰白胎，青釉略泛灰，内施满釉，外施釉至腹下部。（羊泽林）

Fragment of Shizhai kiln celadon bowl

Yuan dynasty, Overall height 8.5cm mouth diameter 13.7cm foot diameter 5.3cm, The Institute of Cultural Relics and Archaeology of the Fujian Museum

020 石寨窑青釉碗残件

元

高 6.2 厘米　口径 14.4 厘米　足径 5.2 厘米

福建博物院文物考古研究所藏

碗圆唇，撇口，深弧腹，圈足。灰白胎，青釉偏灰，内施满釉，外施釉至腹下部，釉面开片。（羊泽林）

Fragment of Shizhai kiln celadon bowl

Yuan dynasty, Height 6.2cm mouth diameter 14.4cm foot diameter 5.2cm, The Institute of Cultural Relics and Archaeology of the Fujian Museum

021 石寨窑青釉盘残件

元

高 5.2 厘米　口径 20.1 厘米　足径 7.3 厘米

福建博物院文物考古研究所藏

盘圆唇，撇口，折沿，斜弧腹，圈足。灰白胎。内施满釉，外施釉至腹下部，部分流釉至足部，青绿色釉，釉面部分有开片。（羊泽林）

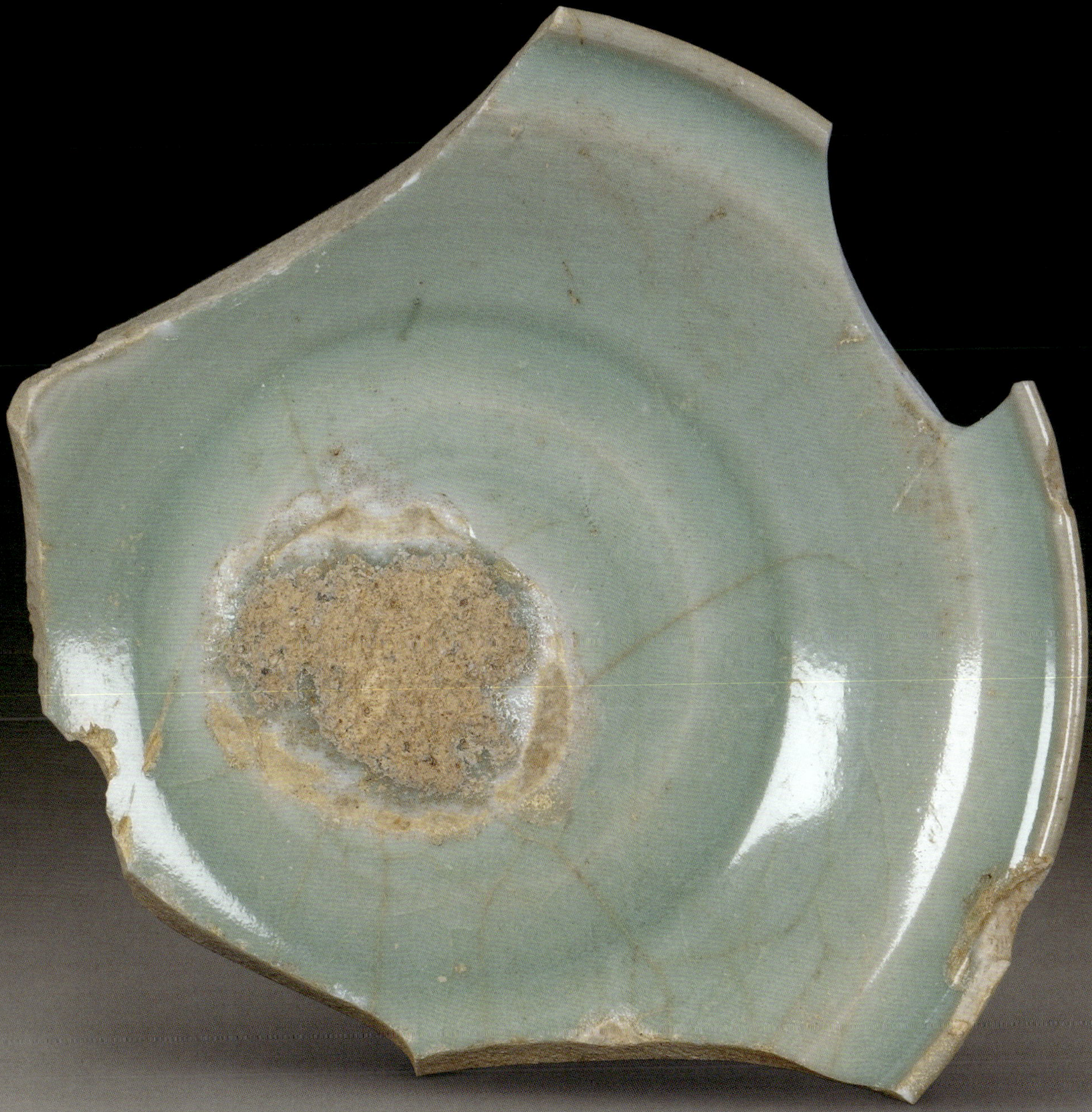

Fragment of Shizhai kiln celadon dish

Yuan dynasty, Height 5.2cm mouth diameter 20.1cm foot diameter 7.3cm, The Institute of Cultural Relics and Archaeology of the Fujian Museum

022 通坑窑青釉刻菊瓣纹碗残件

明

高 5.3 厘米　口径 13.7 厘米　足径 5.7 厘米

南靖县博物馆藏

碗圆唇，敞口，深弧腹，圈足。灰白胎。内施满釉，外施釉至足部，釉色青绿，釉面布满开片。外壁刻菊瓣纹。（张立丽）

Fragment of Tongkeng kiln celadon bowl carved with chrysanthemum petals design

Ming dynasty, Height 5.3cm mouth diameter 13.7cm foot diameter 5.7cm, The Nanjing County Museum

023 通坑窑青釉刻菊瓣纹碗残件

明

高 5.3 厘米　口径 12 厘米　足径 6.2 厘米

南靖县博物馆藏

碗圆唇，敞口，深弧腹，圈足。灰白色胎。内施满釉，外施釉至腹底部，釉色青绿，釉面布满开片。外壁刻菊瓣纹。（张立丽）

Fragment of Tongkeng kiln celadon bowl carved with chrysanthemum petals design

Ming dynasty, Height 5.3cm mouth diameter 12cm foot diameter 6.2cm, The Nanjing County Museum

024 通坑窑青釉碗残件

明

高 3.6 厘米　口径 14 厘米　足径 5.5 厘米

南靖县博物馆藏

碗圆唇，撇口，深折腹，圈足较宽。灰白色胎。内施满釉，口沿内侧有缩釉现象，外壁施釉至足部，釉色青绿泛黄，釉面布满开片。（张立丽）

Fragment of Tongkeng kiln celadon bowl

Ming dynasty, Height 3.6cm mouth diameter 14cm foot diameter 5.5cm, The Nanjing County Museum

025 封门坑窑青釉盘残件

清

高 2.2 厘米　口径 10.2 厘米　足径 4.8 厘米

南靖县博物馆藏

盘敞口，浅腹，圈足。灰白色胎，内、外均施釉，足端刮釉。釉色青绿略泛灰，釉面布满开片。（张立丽）

Fragment of Fengmenkeng kiln celadon dish

Qing dynasty, Height 2.2cm mouth diameter 10.2cm foot diameter 4.8cm, The Nanjing County Museum

026 封门坑窑青釉罐残件（套烧粘连）

清

高 8.5 厘米　口径 11 厘米　足径 9 厘米

南靖县博物馆藏

罐直口，丰肩，鼓腹，下腹内收，圈足。灰胎。罐内施釉至肩上部，外施满釉，足端刮釉。釉色青绿，釉面布满开片。（张立丽）

Fragments of Fengmenkeng kiln celadon jar accidently baked together in the kiln

Qing dynasty, Height 8.5cm mouth diameter 11cm foot diameter 9cm, The Nanjing County Museum

027 封门坑窑青釉水盂残件

清

高 3.5 厘米　口径 1.7 厘米　足径 5 厘米

南靖县博物馆藏

水盂圆唇，敛口，沿内折，斜直腹微弧，卧足。灰白色胎。内施釉至口沿附近，外施釉至腹底部，部分流釉至足部。釉色青绿，釉面布满开片。（张立丽）

Fragment of Fengmenkeng kiln celadon water container

Qing dynasty, Height 3.5cm mouth diameter 1.7cm foot diameter 5cm, The Nanjing County Museum

028

封门坑窑青釉炉残件

清

高 6.3 厘米　口径 8 厘米　足径 4.3 厘米

南靖县博物馆藏

炉微束口，弧腹，圈足，双耳已残。灰胎。内施釉至口沿附近，外施釉至足外墙。釉色青绿泛灰，釉面布满开片。（张立丽）

Fragment of Fengmenkeng kiln celadon incense burner

Qing dynasty, Height 6.3cm mouth diameter 8cm foot diameter 4.3cm, The Nanjing County Museum

029 封门坑窑青釉刻划缠枝牡丹纹三足炉

清

高 14.2 厘米　口径 15.2 厘米

南靖县博物馆藏

炉撇口，束颈，鼓腹，小平底，三乳足。灰胎。内施釉至口沿附近，外施满釉，足底无釉。釉色青绿泛灰。腹部刻划缠枝牡丹纹。（张立丽）

Fengmenkeng kiln celadon tripod incense burner with carved and incised peony scrolls design

Qing dynasty, Height 14.2cm mouth diameter 15.2cm, The Nanjing County Museum

030 封门坑窑青釉刻划缠枝牡丹纹三足筒式炉

清

高 13.4 厘米　口径 12.1 厘米

南靖县博物馆藏

炉直口，沿内折，筒形腹，平底，三倒梯形足。灰胎。内施釉至口沿附近，外施满釉，足底无釉。釉色青绿泛灰。腹部刻划缠枝牡丹纹。（张立丽）

Fengmenkeng kiln celadon tripod incense burner with carved and incised peony scrolls design

Qing dynasty, Height 13.4cm mouth diameter 12.1cm, The Nanjing County Museum

031 | 西门窑青釉刻划草叶纹碗

宋

高 5.7 厘米　口径 13.9 厘米　足径 4.7 厘米

松溪县博物馆藏

碗敞口，斜直腹，圈足。内施满釉，外壁施釉至圈足。釉色青绿略泛黄。内壁刻划草叶纹。内底可见四枚支钉。（杨靖伟）

Ximen kiln celadon bowl with carved and incised foliate design

Song dynasty, Height 5.7cm mouth diameter 13.9cm foot diameter 4.7cm, The Songxi County Museum

032 西门窑青釉刻划草叶纹碗

宋

高 7.5 厘米　口径 15.2 厘米　足径 5.1 厘米

松溪县博物馆藏

碗撇口，深弧腹，圈足。内施满釉，外施釉至圈足。釉色青绿略泛黄。内壁刻划草叶纹，外壁刻划篦划纹。（杨靖伟）

Ximen kiln celadon bowl with carved and incised foliate design

Song dynasty, Height 7.5cm mouth diameter 15.2cm foot diameter 5.1cm, The Songxi County Museum

033 西门窑青釉刻划莲花纹盘残件（套烧粘连）

宋

通高 6.4 厘米　口径 14 厘米　足径 4.4 厘米

松溪县博物馆藏

盘二件套烧。敞口，斜折腹，圈足。内施满釉，外施釉至圈足。釉色青绿略泛黄，釉面布满开片。（杨靖伟）

Ximen kiln celadon dish with carved and incised lotus design accidently baked together in the kiln

Song dynasty, Overall height 6.4cm mouth diameter 14cm foot diameter 4.4cm, The Songxi County Museum

034 西门窑青釉水注残件

宋

高 6.9 厘米　口径 3.9 厘米　足径 5.7 厘米

松溪县博物馆藏

水注直口，圆肩，流与柄残，扁鼓腹，平底微内凹。内施满釉，外壁施釉至腹下部。釉色青绿，釉面布满开片。肩部刻划篦划纹。（杨靖伟）

Fragment of Ximen kiln celadon water dropper

Song dynasty, Height 6.9cm mouth diameter 3.9cm foot diameter 5.7cm, The Songxi County Museum

035 西门窑青釉器盖残件

宋

高 2.5 厘米　径 4.7 厘米　底径 2.1 厘米

松溪县博物馆藏

盖短柱形钮，中部略束，盖面微弧，附环形系，实心柱状底。盖面施釉，釉色青绿。盖面刻划条纹。（杨靖伟）

Fragment of Ximen kiln celadon ware cover

Song dynasty, Height 2.5cm diameter 4.7cm bottom diameter 2.1cm, The Songxi County Museum

036 西门窑青釉炉残件（套烧粘连）

宋

高 8.8 厘米　口径 8.2 厘米　足径 5.6 厘米

松溪县博物馆藏

炉三件套烧。口沿外折，直腹，二层台式足。内施釉至腹上部，外施釉至足下部。釉色青绿，釉面布满开片。外壁刻划篦划纹。（杨靖伟）

Fragment of Ximen kiln celadon incense burner accidently baked together in the kiln

Song dynasty, Height 8.8cm mouth diameter 8.2cm foot diameter 5.6cm, The Songxi County Museum

037 西门窑青釉枕残件

宋

残高 12.7 厘米　足径 10.9 厘米

松溪县博物馆藏

枕面呈盘形，一侧略向下，高圈足。内施满釉，外壁施釉至圈足下部。釉色青中泛灰。（杨靖伟）

Fragment of Ximen kiln celadon pillow

Song dynasty, Remaining height 12.7cm foot diameter 10.9cm, The Songxi County Museum

广东地区的仿龙泉青瓷

广东地区仿烧龙泉青瓷在明代得到发展，窑场有惠州市惠东县白马窑和龙门县三洞村窑、阳江市阳春那漠窑、梅州市大埔县余里窑等。产品以青釉刻菊瓣纹碗、团花纹盘、折沿盘、兽足炉等为代表。

Imitations of Longquan Celadon Fired in Guangdong

Copies of Longquan celadon developed in Guangdong during the Ming dynasty. The kilns for such wares include the Baima kilns in Huidong county and the Sandongcun kilns in Longmen county, Huizhou city, the Namo kilns in Yangchun, Yangjiang city, the Yuli kilns in Dapu county, Meizhou city. Representative products include bowls with carved chrysanthemum petal design, dishes with floral medallion design, dishes with everted mouth rim, and incense burners with animal-shaped feet.

038 惠东窑青釉器残件（6 件）

明

故宫博物院藏

惠东窑位于广东省惠州市惠东县，由惠东三官坑窑和白马窑等窑场组成。主要烧造碗、盘、高足杯、缸、器盖等器物，产品以青釉瓷为主，釉色有青绿、青灰、灰黄等。器表常以模印花卉纹和“富”“寿”“正”“清”“龙”等文字以及刻划花卉纹装饰。（王照宇）

Fragments of Huidong kiln celadon ware

Ming dynasty, The Palace Museum

039 惠东窑青釉折沿盘残件

明

故宫博物院藏

盘折沿，浅弧壁，圈足。内外施青釉，釉色青绿，釉面有开片。足端及足内无釉。内壁刻竖条纹，线条欠匀称。（王照宇）

Fragment of Huidong kiln celadon dish with everted rim

Ming dynasty, The Palace Museum

040 三洞村窑青釉器残件（4件）

明

故宫博物院藏

三洞村窑位于广东省惠州市龙门县三洞村，产品以青釉为主，器类有碗、盘、高足杯等。部分器物内底或外底刻“用”“万”“士”“夫”“祥”“福”等字。碗外壁多刻菊瓣纹。部分碗、盘类器的内底无釉。（王照宇）

Fragments of Sandongcun kiln celadon ware
Ming dynasty, The Palace Museum

041 三洞村窑青釉印瑞兽纹花口折沿盘残件（套烧粘连）

明

故宫博物院藏

套烧残件。盘花口，折沿，浅弧壁，圈足。器身施青釉，釉色浅淡，有开片。足端及足内无釉。盘内壁刻线纹，间距不一。内底涩胎无釉，系叠烧处。盘心印瑞兽纹。（王照宇）

Fragment of Sandongcun kiln celadon dish with everted rim and impressed design of auspicious beast accidently baked together in the kiln

Ming dynasty, The Palace Museum

042 那漠窑青釉器残件（2件）

明

故宫博物院藏

那漠窑位于广东省阳春市岗美镇那漠村，产品以青瓷器为主。器物类型有碗、碟、罐、高足杯等。纹饰常见菊瓣纹。胎质较坚硬。部分碗类器内底无釉。（王照宇）

Fragments of Namo kiln celadon ware

Ming dynasty, The Palace Museum

043 那漠窑青釉刻菊瓣纹碗残件

明

故宫博物院藏

碗内壁粘连匣钵底部，足端粘连窑具。器身施青釉，釉色青绿，施釉欠均匀，釉面有开片。足端及足内无釉。碗外壁刻菊瓣纹。（王照宇）

Fragment of Namo kiln celadon dish with everted rim and carved chrysanthemum petals design

Ming dynasty, The Palace Museum

044 余里窑青釉器残件（4 件）

明

故宫博物院藏

余里窑位于广东省梅州市大埔县三河镇余里村，其烧造的青瓷釉色、纹饰和制作工艺均与龙泉青瓷相似。器物造型有罐、双耳瓶、壶、炉、碗、盘、碟、杯、盏、洗、砚等。纹饰常见菊瓣纹、团菊纹、回纹等，碗类器物内底多印有文字，见有“福”“禄”“寿”“安”“然”“富”“宁”“玉”等字。（王照宇）

Fragments of Yuli kiln celadon ware

Ming dynasty, The Palace Museum

045 余里窑青釉罐残件

明中期

高 5.5 厘米　口径 11 厘米　足径 8.3 厘米

广东省文物考古研究所藏

罐敛口，弧腹，圈足。胎质坚硬致密，胎色灰白。通体施青绿色釉，釉薄处发白，积釉处颜色较深，施釉至足底，足内露胎，釉面有开片。外壁、内壁和内底素面。（肖达顺、陈以琴）

Fragment of Yuli kiln celadon jar

Middle Ming dynasty, Height 5.5cm mouth diameter 11cm foot diameter 8.3cm, The Institute of Cultural Relics and Archaeology of Guangdong Province

046 余里窑青釉碗残件

明中期

高 8.6 厘米　口径 16 厘米　足径 7.1 厘米

广东省文物考古研究所藏

碗敞口，深弧腹，圈足。胎质坚硬紧密，灰白胎。内、外施青绿色釉，釉色发白，釉面有开片，施釉至足底，足内露胎。外壁、内壁和内底素面。（肖达顺、陈以琴）

Fragment of Yuli kiln celadon bowl

Middle Ming dynasty, Height 8.6cm mouth diameter 16cm foot diameter 7.1cm, The Institute of Cultural Relics and Archaeology of Guangdong Province

047 余里窑青釉印“安”字刻菊瓣纹碗残件

明中期

高 6.7 厘米　口径 14.2 厘米　足径 6.5 厘米

广东省文物考古研究所藏

碗敞口，深弧腹，圈足。胎质坚硬紧密，灰白胎。通体施青绿色釉，釉色深而发暗，施釉至足底，足内露胎。碗外壁刻双弦菊瓣纹，内壁素面，内底戳印“安”字，围以花瓣。（肖达顺、陈以琴）

Fragment of Yuli kiln celadon bowl with impressed character An and carved chrysanthemum petals design

Middle Ming dynasty, Height 6.7cm mouth diameter 14.2cm foot diameter 6.5cm The Institute of Cultural Relics and Archaeology of Guangdong Province

048 余里窑青釉刻菊瓣纹高足碗残件

明中期

高 9.9 厘米　口径 11 厘米　足径 4.2 厘米

广东省文物考古研究所藏

碗敞口，深弧壁，高足。胎质坚硬致密，灰白胎。通体施青绿色釉，釉色发白，施釉至足底，足内露胎。外壁刻划双弦菊瓣纹，内壁和内底素面。（肖达顺、陈以琴）

Fragment of Yuli kiln celadon bowl with high stem and carved chrysanthemum petals design

Middle Ming dynasty, Height 9.9cm mouth diameter 11cm foot diameter 4.2cm, The Institute of Cultural Relics and Archaeology of Guangdong Province

049 余里窑青釉印海兽纹盘残件

明中期

高 2.9 厘米　口径 10.7 厘米　足径 6.3 厘米

广东省文物考古研究所藏

盘敞口，浅弧腹，圈足。胎质粗松，黄白色胎。内、外施青灰色釉，釉色发白，釉面有开片，外壁施釉至足底，足内露胎。外壁素面，内底刻单圈弦纹，圈内刻海兽波涛纹，内壁刻竖条纹。（肖达顺、陈以琴）

Fragment of Yuli kiln celadon dish with design of impressed sea monster

Middle Ming dynasty, Height 2.9cm mouth diameter 10.7cm foot diameter 6.3cm, The Institute of Cultural Relics and Archaeology of Guangdong Province

050 余里窑青釉印“安”字盘残件

明中期

高 2.7 厘米　口径 10.6 厘米　足径 6.1 厘米

广东省文物考古研究所藏

盘敞口，浅弧腹，圈足。胎质坚硬致密，青灰色胎。通体施深绿色釉，釉面有开片。施釉至足底，足内露胎。外壁素面，内壁刻竖条纹，内底印“安”字，外围花瓣。（肖达顺、陈以琴）

Fragment of Yuli kiln celadon dish with impressed character An

Middle Ming dynasty, Height 2.7cm mouth diameter 10.6cm foot diameter 6.1cm, The Institute of Cultural Relics and Archaeology of Guangdong Province

051 余里窑青釉印“宁”字盘残件

明中期

高 3.1 厘米　口径 10.4 厘米　足径 6 厘米

广东省文物考古研究所藏

盘敞口，浅弧腹，圈足。胎质坚硬，夹砂，黄白色胎。内外施青绿色釉，施釉至足底，底内露胎。外壁有修胎痕，内壁刻竖条纹，内底中心印“宁”字，外刻一周弦纹。（肖达顺、陈以琴）

Fragment of Yuli kiln celadon dish with impressed character Ning

Middle Ming dynasty, Height 3.1cm mouth diameter 10.4cm foot diameter 6cm, The Institute of Cultural Relics and Archaeology of Guangdong Province

052 余里窑青釉刻竖条纹折沿盘残件

明中期

高 3.7 厘米　口径 18 厘米　足径 8.2 厘米

广东省文物考古研究所藏

盘撇口，宽沿，浅弧腹，圈足。胎质坚硬致密，灰白胎。通体施深绿色釉，釉薄处发白，积釉处颜色较深，施釉至足底，足内露胎。外壁素面，内壁刻竖条纹，内底以中心为圆点刻螺旋纹，螺旋纹外刻单圈弦纹。（肖达顺、陈以琴）

Fragment of Yuli kiln celadon dish with everted rim and carved with lines design

Middle Ming dynasty, Height 3.7cm mouth diameter 18cm foot diameter 8.2cm, The Institute of Cultural Relics and Archaeology of Guangdong Province

053 余里窑青釉折腰盘残件

明中期

高 3.5 厘米　口径 14.7 厘米　足径 6.8 厘米

广东省文物考古研究所藏

盘撇口，浅腹，圈足。胎质坚硬致密，灰白胎。通体施青灰色釉，釉色发白，施釉至底，圈足露胎。外壁、内壁和内底素面。（肖达顺、陈以琴）

Fragment of Yuli kiln celadon dish with angled wall

Middle Ming dynasty, Height 3.5cm mouth diameter 14.7cm foot diameter 6.8cm, The Institute of Cultural Relics and Archaeology of Guangdong Province

054 余里窑青釉碟残件

明中期

高 1.5 厘米　口径 8.6 厘米　足径 4.6 厘米

广东省文物考古研究所藏

碟敞口，斜直腹，平底。胎质坚硬致密，灰白胎。施浅绿色釉，釉薄处发白，积釉处颜色较深，施釉至下腹部，釉面有开片。外壁、内壁和内底素面。（肖达顺、陈以琴）

Fragment of Yuli kiln celadon saucer

Middle Ming dynasty, Height 1.5cm mouth diameter 8.6cm foot diameter 4.6cm, The Institute of Cultural Relics and Archaeology of Guangdong Province

055 余里窑青釉刻菊瓣纹高足碗残件

明

故宫博物院藏

碗圆唇，敞口，深弧腹，高足。柄中部束收。内外施青釉，釉色青绿，釉层较均匀。足端及足内无釉。口沿下刻一周回纹，腹部刻菊瓣纹，柄中部刻三道弦纹。（王照宇）

Fragment of Yuli kiln celadon dish with high stem and carved chrysanthemum petals design

Ming dynasty, The Palace Museum

江西地区的仿龙泉青瓷

江西地区烧造仿龙泉青瓷的窑场主要有景德镇窑、抚州市塘尾窑、上饶市上窑口窑等。明代景德镇御器厂和民窑亦均烧造仿龙泉青瓷。宣德时期，景德镇御器厂烧造的青瓷不仅釉色接近龙泉青瓷，部分器物在装烧工艺上也采用与龙泉青瓷相同的外底刮釉垫烧的方式。正统、景泰、天顺时期，景德镇御器厂的青瓷烧造工艺已非常成熟，这类青瓷成为御窑瓷器的重要品种。

Imitations of Longquan Celadon Fired in Jiangxi

The kilns firing copies of Longquan celadon in Jiangxi primarily include the Jingdezhen kilns, the Tangwei kilns in Fuzhou city, and the Shangyaokou (lit. 'the upper kilns') kilns in Shangrao city. During the Ming dynasty, both the Imperial Ware Workshop and private kilns in Jingdezhen fired Longquan style celadon. In the reign of the Xuande emperor, the celadon made in the imperial kilns are similar to Longquan wares not only in glaze, but also in techniques of setting in kiln for some objects, such as removing part of glaze from their external base to avoid sticking with setters. By the reign periods of Zhengtong, Jingtai and Tianshun, the celadon firing techniques already fully matured in the imperial kilns of Jingdezhen, and celadon became a significant type among its products.

056 景德镇窑青釉高足碗

明永乐

高 12.3 厘米　口径 16.3 厘米　足径 4.6 厘米

清宫旧藏

故宫博物院藏

碗撇口，深弧腹，瘦底，底下承以外撇高足。高足自下往上三分之二处饰一道凸弦纹。碗内、外和高足内均施翠青釉，足端无釉，系垫饼垫烧部位。（单莹莹）

Jingdezhen kiln celadon bowl with high stem

Yongle period, Ming dynasty, Height 12.3cm mouth diameter 16.3cm foot diameter 4.6cm, Collected by the Qing Palace, The Palace Museum

附 1　龙泉窑青釉高足碗

元

高 9 厘米　口径 9.5 厘米　足径 3.7 厘米

故宫博物院藏

碗撇口，深弧腹，瘦底，底下承以中空高足。碗内、外和高足内均施青灰色釉。足中间凸起一道弦纹。（董健丽）

Longquan celadon bowl with high stem

Yuan dynasty, Height 9cm mouth diameter 9.5cm foot diameter 3.7cm, The Palace Museum

057 景德镇窑青釉三系盖罐

明永乐

高 10.4 厘米　口径 9.9 厘米　足径 14.1 厘米

清宫旧藏

故宫博物院藏

罐直口，溜肩，鼓腹，平底，圈足。罐内施透明釉，外壁施翠青釉，足端无釉。肩部均匀置三个圆环形系，三系各有一花形托。罐附钖锣形盖。（单莹莹）

Jingdezhen kiln celadon covered jar with three handles

Yongle period, Ming dynasty, Height 10.4cm mouth diameter 9.9cm foot diameter 14.1cm, Collected by the Qing Palace, The Palace Museum

058 景德镇窑青釉葵口盘

明宣德

高 4 厘米　口径 17.5 厘米　足径 11 厘米

故宫博物院藏

盘外撇葵口，浅弧壁，圈足。盘内、外和圈足内均施青釉。足底无釉。外底署青花楷体“大明宣德年制”六字双行外围双圈款。（孙悦）

Jingdezhen kiln celadon dish with sunflower shaped rim

Xuande period, Ming dynasty, Height 4cm mouth diameter 17.5cm foot diameter 11cm, The Palace Museum

059 景德镇窑青釉刻划花卉纹菱花口折腰碟

明宣德

高 2.9 厘米　口径 8.7 厘米　足径 4.3 厘米

清宫旧藏

故宫博物院藏

碟外撇菱花口，浅弧壁，折腰，圈足。内、外和圈足内均施青釉，足底无釉。碟内壁刻划花卉纹，内底署青花楷体“大明宣德年制”六字双行款，字体为明初书法家沈度的“台阁体”。

明初自永乐朝开始，景德镇御器厂开始大量仿烧龙泉青瓷，造型主要有碗、罐、盘、碟、高足杯等，其釉色稍偏青绿，系因胎体比龙泉窑青瓷胎体更白所致。（孙悦）

Jingdezhen kiln celadon saucer with everted bracket-lobed rim and angled wall and carved and incised floral design

Xuande period, Ming dynasty, Height 2.9cm mouth diameter 8.7cm foot diameter 4.3cm, Collected by the Qing Palace, The Palace Museum

060 景德镇窑青釉刻划花卉纹菱花口折腰碟

明宣德

高 2.9 厘米　口径 8.7 厘米　足径 4.3 厘米

清宫旧藏

故宫博物院藏

碟外撇菱花口，浅弧壁，折腰，圈足。内、外和圈足内均施青釉，足底无釉。内壁刻划花卉纹，内底署青花楷体“大明宣德年制”六字双行款。（孙悦）

Jingdezhen kiln celadon saucer with everted bracket-lobed rim and angled wall and carved and incised floral design

Xuande period, Ming dynasty, Height 2.9cm mouth diameter 8.7cm foot diameter 4.3cm, Collected by the Qing Palace, The Palace Museum

大明宣德年製

061 景德镇窑青釉刻缠枝莲纹碗

明

高 6.9 厘米　口径 15.4 厘米　足径 5 厘米

清宫旧藏

故宫博物院藏

碗撇口，深弧腹，瘦底，圈足。碗内、外和圈足内均施青釉，釉层厚薄不均。足端无釉，系垫饼垫烧部位，露出白色胎体。外壁刻六组缠枝莲纹，圈足外墙亦刻花卉边饰，口沿下和足墙下部均刻两道弦纹。（单莹莹）

Jingdezhen kiln celadon bowl carved with lotus scrolls design

Ming dynasty, Height 6.9cm mouth diameter 15.4cm foot diameter 5cm, Collected by the Qing Palace, The Palace Museum

062 景德镇窑青釉刻“寿”字折沿盘

明

高 5.5 厘米　口径 26 厘米　足径 13.5 厘米

故宫博物院藏

盘敞口，折沿，浅弧壁，圈足。内、外和圈足内均施青釉，釉面莹润光亮。外底有一圈涩胎无釉，呈火石红色，系垫圈垫烧处。内底刻一“寿”字，内壁刻划七道弦纹，外壁光素。（张涵）

Jingdezhen kiln celadon dish with everted rim and carved character Shou

Ming dynasty, Height 5.5cm mouth diameter 26cm foot diameter 13.5cm, The Palace Museum

063 景德镇窑青釉刻花瓣纹花口盘

明

高 3 厘米　口径 19.5 厘米　足径 10.5 厘米

故宫博物院藏

盘敞口，浅斜腹，厚唇，圈足，口作花瓣形。内、外施青釉，釉面玻璃质感较强，且遍布细碎开片。内底刻花瓣纹，内壁刻鱼鳞纹。胎体厚重，外底、足端皆无釉，露出灰色胎。（蒋艺）

Jingdezhen kiln celadon dish with everted lobed rim and carved floral design

Ming dynasty, Height 3cm mouth diameter 19.5cm foot diameter 10.5cm, The Palace Museum

064 景德镇窑青釉刻花瓣纹菱花口折沿盘

明

高 5.5 厘米　口径 31.5 厘米　足径 15.5 厘米

故宫博物院藏

盘敞口，折沿，厚唇，斜弧腹，圈足，口作菱花形。通体施青釉。内底刻花瓣纹，内壁印竖条纹。外底施白釉，足端无釉，露出灰白色胎。（蒋艺）

Jingdezhen kiln celadon dish with everted bracket-lobed rim and carved floral petals design

Ming dynasty, Height 5.5cm mouth diameter 31.5cm foot diameter 15.5cm, The Palace Museum

065 景德镇窑青釉刻花瓣纹菱花口折沿盘

明

高 3.2 厘米　口径 20.3 厘米　足径 9.7 厘米

故宫博物院藏

盘敞口，折沿，浅弧腹，圈足，口作菱花形。通体施青釉，釉色翠青。内底刻花瓣形纹，内壁刻划鱼鳞纹。胎体厚重，外底、足端皆无釉，露出灰白色胎体。（蒋艺）

Jingdezhen kiln celadon dish with everted bracket-lobed rim and carved floral petals design

Ming dynasty, Height 3.2cm mouth diameter 20.3cm foot diameter 9.7cm, The Palace Museum

故宫博物院

066 景德镇窑青釉篦划花纹八方盘

明

高 4 厘米　口径 18.2 厘米　足径 8 厘米

故宫博物院藏

盘呈八方形，敞口，浅壁，圈足。足端和外底不施釉，余处施青釉。内底有篦划纹饰，内壁依造型分为八个开光，开光内均以篦划纹装饰，外壁亦饰篦划花纹。图案简单、随意。（张涵）

Jingdezhen kiln celadon octagonal dish with incised design

Ming dynasty, Height 4cm mouth diameter 18.2cm foot diameter 8cm, The Palace Museum

067 景德镇窑青釉刻划缠枝花纹直颈瓶

清康熙

高 25 厘米　口径 3.4 厘米　足径 6.4 厘米

故宫博物院藏

瓶撇口，长直径，溜肩，圆鼓腹，圈足。外壁通体施青釉，瓶腹部刻划缠枝花纹。瓶内和圈足内均施透明釉，圈底无釉，露出浅黄色胎。(孙悦)

Jingdezhen kiln celadon vase with straight neck and carved and incised floral scrolls design

Kangxi period, Qing dynasty, Height 25cm mouth diameter 3.4cm foot diameter 6.4cm, The Palace Museum

068 景德镇窑青釉刻划缠枝花纹直颈瓶

清康熙

高 25.8 厘米　口径 4.2 厘米　足径 8 厘米

清宫旧藏

故宫博物院藏

瓶直口，圆唇，长直颈，溜肩，圆鼓腹，圈足外撇。外壁通体施青釉，足底无釉。颈中部饰一道凸弦纹，肩部饰两道凸弦纹，颈部凸弦纹处刻莲瓣纹，腹部刻划缠枝花纹。瓶内和圈足内均施透明釉。(孙悦)

Jingdezhen kiln celadon vase with straight neck and carved and incised floral scrolls design

Kangxi period, Qing dynasty, Height 25.8cm mouth diameter 4.2cm foot diameter 8cm, Collected by the Qing Palace, The Palace Museum

069 景德镇窑青釉刻蕉叶纹觚

清康熙

高 23.5 厘米　口径 12.3 厘米

清宫旧藏

故宫博物院藏

觚仿商周青铜器造型。敞口，直壁，腹部微鼓，足胫处微外撇，圈足。通体施豆青色釉。腹部上下各刻两道弦纹，将花觚主题纹饰分为三层。颈部和胫部均为蕉叶纹，腹部为如意头纹。花觚内及圈足内均施透明釉，足底无釉。（孙悦）

Jingdezhen kiln celadon vase with flanges in form of an archaistic bronze *gu* and carved plantain leaves design

Kangxi period, Qing dynasty, Height 23.5cm mouth diameter 12.3cm, Collected by the Qing Palace, The Palace Museum

070 景德镇窑青釉刻云龙缠枝莲纹碗

清康熙

高 6.9 厘米　口径 15 厘米　足径 6.1 厘米

清宫旧藏

故宫博物院藏

碗撇口，深弧腹，圈足。内、外和圈足内均施青釉，釉色翠青。内壁锥拱赶珠龙纹，内底锥拱云气纹，外壁锥拱缠枝莲纹。外底署青花楷体“大清康熙年制”六字双行外围双圈款。足端无釉，露出白色胎体。（蒋艺）

Jingdezhen kiln celadon bowl carved with design of dragon, cloud and lotus scrolls

Kangxi period, Qing dynasty, Height 6.9cm mouth diameter 15cm foot diameter 6.1cm, Collected by the Qing Palace, The Palace Museum

071 景德镇窑青釉刻如意头纹盘

清康熙

高 3.2 厘米　口径 11.1 厘米　足径 5.5 厘米

故宫博物院藏

盘敞口，浅弧腹，圈足。内、外均施青釉，釉色翠青。足端无釉，露白色胎体。外壁上腹部凸刻如意头纹，近底处凸刻仰莲瓣纹。圈足内施透明釉。外底署青花楷体“大清康熙年制”六字双行外围双圈款。（蒋艺）

Jingdezhen kiln celadon dish carved with Ruyi-head design

Kangxi period, Qing dynasty, Height 3.2cm mouth diameter 11.1cm foot diameter 5.5cm, The Palace Museum

072 景德镇窑青釉刻云纹菱花口盘

清康熙

高 3.9 厘米　口径 13 厘米　足径 6.7 厘米

故宫博物院藏

盘菱花口外撇，浅弧壁，圈足。内、外和圈足内均施青釉，足底无釉。内外壁均刻云纹。内底方形开光内署青花楷体“大清康熙年制”六字双行款。冬青釉系康熙朝仿龙泉釉中的一种。（孙悦）

Jingdezhen kiln celadon dish with everted bracket-lobed rim and carved cloud design

Kangxi period, Qing dynasty, Height 3.9cm mouth diameter 13cm foot diameter 6.7cm, The Palace Museum

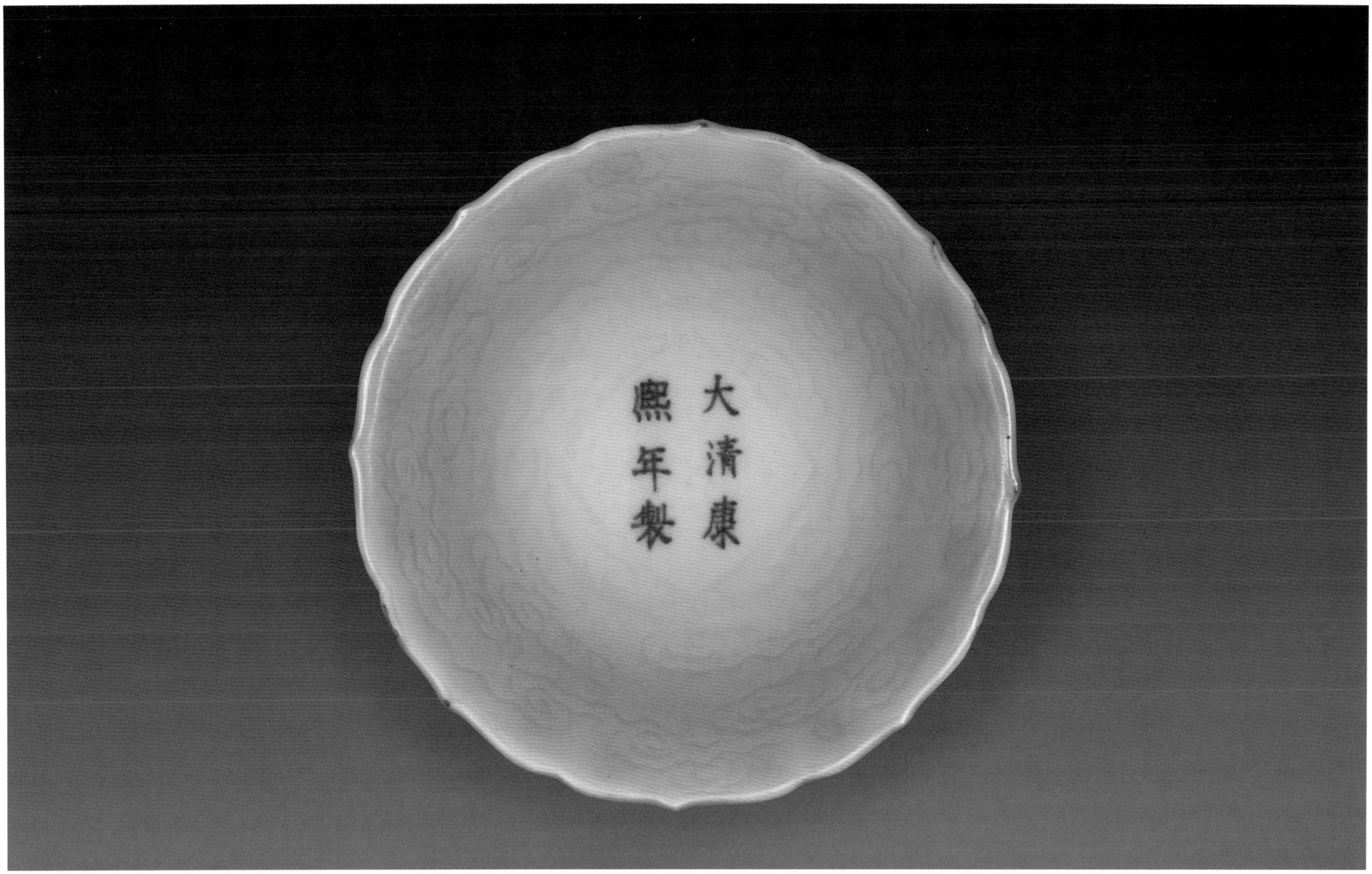
大清康
熙年製

073 景德镇窑青釉折沿洗

清康熙

高 8 厘米　口径 38.8 厘米　足径 29.8 厘米

清宫旧藏

故宫博物院藏

洗折沿，斜直壁，圈足。内、外通体施青釉，圈足内施透明釉。外底中心署青花楷体“大清康熙年制”六字双行外围双圈款。足底无釉。

折沿洗为龙泉窑青瓷典型器形，自宋代开始便很流行。关于其用途，有盥洗器、文房器笔洗、宗教仪式中的净手器等不同说法。（孙悦）

Jingdezhen kiln celadon washer with everted rim

Kangxi period, Qing dynasty, Height 8cm mouth diameter 38.8cm foot diameter 29.8cm, Collected by the Qing Palace, The Palace Museum

074 景德镇窑青釉刻缠枝牡丹纹玉壶春瓶

清雍正

高 32.5 厘米　口径 9.7 厘米　足径 11.5 厘米

清宫旧藏

故宫博物院藏

瓶撇口，束颈，垂腹，圈足。瓶内、外和圈足内均施青釉，足底涂酱色釉。外壁自上而下依次刻划蕉叶纹、回纹、卷草纹、如意头纹、缠枝牡丹纹、变形莲瓣纹等。腹中部的缠枝牡丹纹为主题纹饰。

玉壶春瓶为宋元时期流行的酒瓶式样，明清时期亦大量烧造，器形较宋元时期略显浑厚。（孙悦）

Jingdezhen kiln celadon *yuhuchun* ('spring in a jade bottle') vase carved with peony scrolls design

Yongzheng period, Qing dynasty, Height 32.5cm mouth diameter 9.7cm foot diameter 11.5cm, Collected by the Qing Palace, The Palace Museum

075 景德镇窑青釉贯耳委角四方瓶

清雍正

高 13.4 厘米　口横 5 厘米　口纵 4 厘米

足横 5.1 厘米　足纵 4.1 厘米

清宫旧藏

故宫博物院藏

瓶呈四方委角形。撇口，垂腹，四方委角圈足，肩部两侧对称置管状耳。内、外施冬青釉，釉色青翠，圈足内施透明釉。足底无釉，外底署青花篆体“雍正年制”四字双行款。

贯耳瓶造型源自汉代流行的青铜投壶式样。清代御窑烧造的贯耳瓶，一般作为陈设器或花瓶使用。（孙悦）

Jingdezhen kiln celadon square vase with tubular handles

Yongzheng period, Qing dynasty, Height 13.4cm mouth length 5cm mouth width 4cm foot length 5.1cm foot width 4.1cm, Collected by the Qing Palace, The Palace Museum

076 景德镇窑青釉琮式瓶

清雍正

高 35.5 厘米　口径 13 厘米　足径 15 厘米

故宫博物院藏

瓶仿玉琮造型。直口，方腹，圈足。瓶内、外和圈足内均施青釉，底足无釉。外壁四面均雕刻凸起的出筋。

早在宋代，瓷器就已开始出现仿玉琮造型。清代沿袭明代“祭器皆用瓷”的规定，制作了大量仿铜、玉器造型的瓷器，用于皇家祭祀活动或宫殿陈设。（孙悦）

Jingdezhen kiln celadon vase inspired by a Neolithic ritual jade *cong*

Yongzheng period, Qing dynasty, Height 35.5cm mouth diameter 13cm foot diameter 15cm, The Palace Museum

附 2　龙泉窑青釉琮式瓶

南宋

高 42 厘米　口径 11.4 厘米　足径 11.4 厘米

清宫旧藏

故宫博物院藏

瓶仿古玉琮造型。敛口，短颈，平肩，方形直腹，圈足。口与足大小相若。瓶内、外和圈足内均施青釉，釉色温润，釉层肥腴。足端不施釉，露胎表面呈火石红色。清宫收藏的宋代官窑、汝窑、龙泉窑瓷器，一直是清代御窑厂仿烧的对象，其美丽的釉色和优美的造型成为追求的艺术目标。（王照宇）

Longquan celadon vase inspired by a Neolithic ritual jade *cong*

Southern Song dynasty, Height 42cm mouth diameter 11.4cm foot diameter 11.4cm, Collected by the Qing Palace, The Palace Museum

077 景德镇窑青釉刻缠枝莲纹碗

清雍正

高 6.5 厘米　口径 16.5 厘米　足径 6 厘米

清宫旧藏

故宫博物院藏

碗撇口，深弧腹，圈足。内、外施冬青釉，外壁刻划缠枝莲纹。圈足内施青釉，足底无釉。外底中心署青花楷体“大清雍正年制”六字双行外围双圈款。（孙悦）

Jingdezhen kiln celadon bowl carved with lotus scrolls design

Yongzheng period, Qing dynasty, Height 6.5cm mouth diameter 16.5cm foot diameter 6cm, Collected by the Qing Palace, The Palace Museum

078 景德镇窑青釉刻缠枝牡丹纹碗

清雍正

高 12.6 厘米　口径 27 厘米　足径 12 厘米

清宫旧藏

故宫博物院藏

碗敞口，深弧腹，圈足。内、外施青釉。外壁凸刻缠枝牡丹纹，近口沿处凸刻夔纹，圈足外墙刻划回纹，内底刻划牡丹纹。圈足内施透明釉，足底无釉。外底署青花篆体“大清雍正年制”六字三行款。（孙悦）

Jingdezhen kiln celadon bowl carved with peony scrolls design

Yongzheng period, Qing dynasty, Height 12.6cm mouth diameter 27cm foot diameter 12cm, Collected by the Qing Palace, The Palace Museum

079 景德镇窑青釉印菊瓣纹折沿盘

清雍正

高 3 厘米　口径 17.5 厘米　足径 11 厘米

清宫旧藏

故宫博物院藏

盘呈菊花式。敞口，折沿，浅弧壁，圈足。内、外施青釉，圈足内施透明釉。外底中心署青花楷体“大清雍正年制”六字双行外围双圈款。

据内务府造办处档案记载，雍正十一年十二月二十七日，“内务府总管年希尧家人郑天锡送来……各式菊花式磁盘十二色（内每色一件）……奉旨：着交与烧造磁器处照此样式每色烧造四十件，钦此”。由此可知，此类相同造型的菊花式盘在雍正朝烧造甚多，且有 12 种不同釉色。这件青釉菊花式盘，即是其中之一。（孙悦）

Jingdezhen kiln celadon dish with everted rim and impressed chrysanthemum petals design

Yongzheng period, Qing dynasty, Height 3cm mouth diameter 17.5cm foot diameter 11cm, Collected by the Qing Palace, The Palace Museum

故宮博物院點訖
482
第7549號
留平物品新號

附 3　龙泉窑青釉印折枝牡丹纹菊瓣式盘

明早期

高 5.7 厘米　口径 33.3 厘米　足径 21 厘米

故宫博物院藏

盘呈菊瓣式。敞口，浅弧腹，圈足。盘内、外和圈足内均施青釉，釉面莹润光亮。外底有涩圈，系垫圈垫烧处。内底印一株折枝牡丹。

此盘形体较大，从造型和纹饰看，应属于明代早期龙泉窑烧造的宫廷用瓷。（黄卫文）

Longquan celadon chrysanthemum dish with impressed peony spray design

Early Ming dynasty, Height 5.7cm mouth diameter 33.3cm foot diameter 21cm, The Palace Museum

080 景德镇窑青釉荷叶式洗

清雍正

高 7 厘米　口径 37 厘米　足距 30 厘米

故宫博物院藏

洗呈半开荷叶形。平底。内、外施仿龙泉青釉，釉色葱翠，釉面有细碎开片，釉下刻荷叶筋脉，显得生动自然。

洗为文房用具。此洗造型别致，做工精细，体现出雍正朝青釉瓷的烧造水平。（陈润民）

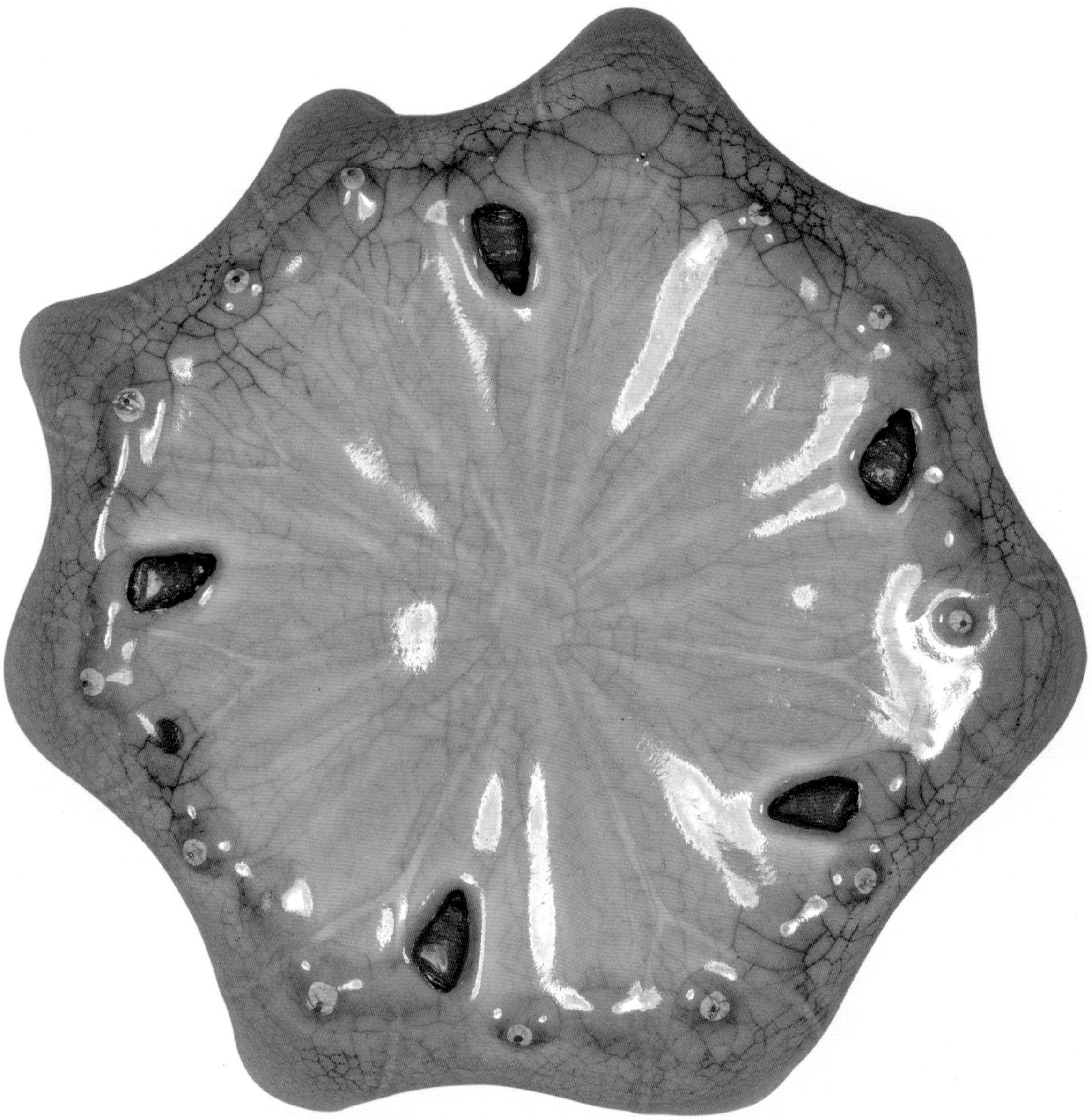

Jingdezhen kiln celadon washer in shape of lotus leaf

Yongzheng period, Qing dynasty, Height 7cm mouth diameter 37cm distance between feet 30cm, The Palace Museum

081 景德镇窑青釉鬲式炉

清雍正

高 13.5 厘米　口径 15.8 厘米　足距 7.5 厘米

清宫旧藏

故宫博物院藏

炉折沿，阔颈，扁圆腹，肩上凸起一周弦纹，下承以三根圆柱形足。内、外施青釉。此炉造型古朴，釉质温润，体现出雍正朝仿南宋龙泉青瓷的最高水平。（陈润民）

Jingdezhen kiln celadon incense burner in form of an archaistic bronze *li*

Yongzheng period, Qing dynasty, Height 13.5cm mouth diameter 15.8cm distance between feet 7.5cm, Collected by the Qing Palace, The Palace Museum

082 景德镇窑青釉鬲式炉

清雍正

高 13.5 厘米　口径 15.8 厘米　足距 7 厘米

清宫旧藏

故宫博物院藏

炉折沿，阔颈，扁圆腹，下承以三根圆柱状足。内、外施青釉，釉色晶莹温润，深浅适中。此炉反映出雍正朝高超的青釉瓷烧造水平。（陈润民）

Jingdezhen kiln celadon incense burner in form of an archaistic bronze *li*

Yongzheng period, Qing dynasty, Height 13.5cm mouth diameter 15.8cm distance between feet 7cm, Collected by the Qing Palace, The Palace Museum

附 4 龙泉窑青釉出筋鬲式炉

南宋

高 9.6 厘米　口径 12.1 厘米　足距 8.2 厘米

清宫旧藏

故宫博物院藏

此炉造型仿青铜鬲，因此又称鬲式炉。折沿，阔颈，扁圆腹，下承以三足。肩部饰凸起弦纹一道，腹部与三足对应处饰有三条凸起的直线纹，俗称“出筋”。通体施青绿色釉，三足底部无釉处显露酱黄色。

炉腹至足部凸起的三条棱线原系仿青铜鬲纹饰，因凸起处釉层较薄，故呈浅白色，形成出筋效果。（赵小春）

Longquan celadon incense burner in form of an archaistic bronze *li*

Southern Song dynasty, Height 9.6cm mouth diameter 12.1cm distance between feet 8.2cm, Collected by the Qing Palace, The Palace Museum

083 景德镇窑青釉刻划缠枝牡丹纹梅瓶

清乾隆

高 41 厘米　口径 5.4 厘米　足径 12 厘米

清宫旧藏

故宫博物院藏

瓶直口，短颈，丰肩，鼓腹，腹下渐收敛，瓶圈足。内、外和圈足内皆施仿龙泉青釉，足内无釉露胎，外底刮釉仅留中心一撮釉。瓶附钟形盖，盖顶置花苞形钮。外壁肩腹部刻划缠枝牡丹纹，近足处刻划变形莲瓣纹。此瓶造型端庄、纹饰优美，具有很高的欣赏价值。（陈润民）

Jingdezhen kiln celadon *meiping* ('prunus vase') with carved and incised peony scrolls design

Qianlong period, Qing dynasty, Height 41cm mouth diameter 5.4cm foot diameter 12cm, Collected by the Qing Palace, The Palace Museum

084 景德镇窑青釉镂空缠枝牡丹纹玉壶春式套瓶

清乾隆

高 32.5 厘米　口径 5 厘米　足径 10 厘米

清宫旧藏

故宫博物院藏

瓶撇口，长颈，溜肩，垂腹，圈足外撇。内、外和圈足内均施青釉，釉色粉青，釉面温润。足端无釉，露出白灰色胎。近口沿处刻一周如意头纹，颈上部刻划仰蕉叶纹，下部刻如意头纹。腹部镂空缠枝牡丹纹，近足处刻仰莲瓣纹。外底署青花篆体“大清乾隆年制”六字三行款。此瓶为套瓶，透过镂空处可见瓶内有一胆，内胆亦施青釉。

镂空工艺是龙泉窑的典型工艺，多用于器座和香薰装饰。在 1976 年韩国新安海域元代沉船打捞出水的龙泉窑瓷器中，就有多件元代龙泉窑青釉镂空瓶。但是外镂孔、内有胆的工艺，在中国最早见于南宋老虎洞窑址出土的玉壶春式瓶和三足樽式炉，这种工艺极可能是受波斯工艺的影响。此瓶为清代乾隆朝景德镇御窑厂仿烧的龙泉釉产品。(蒋艺)

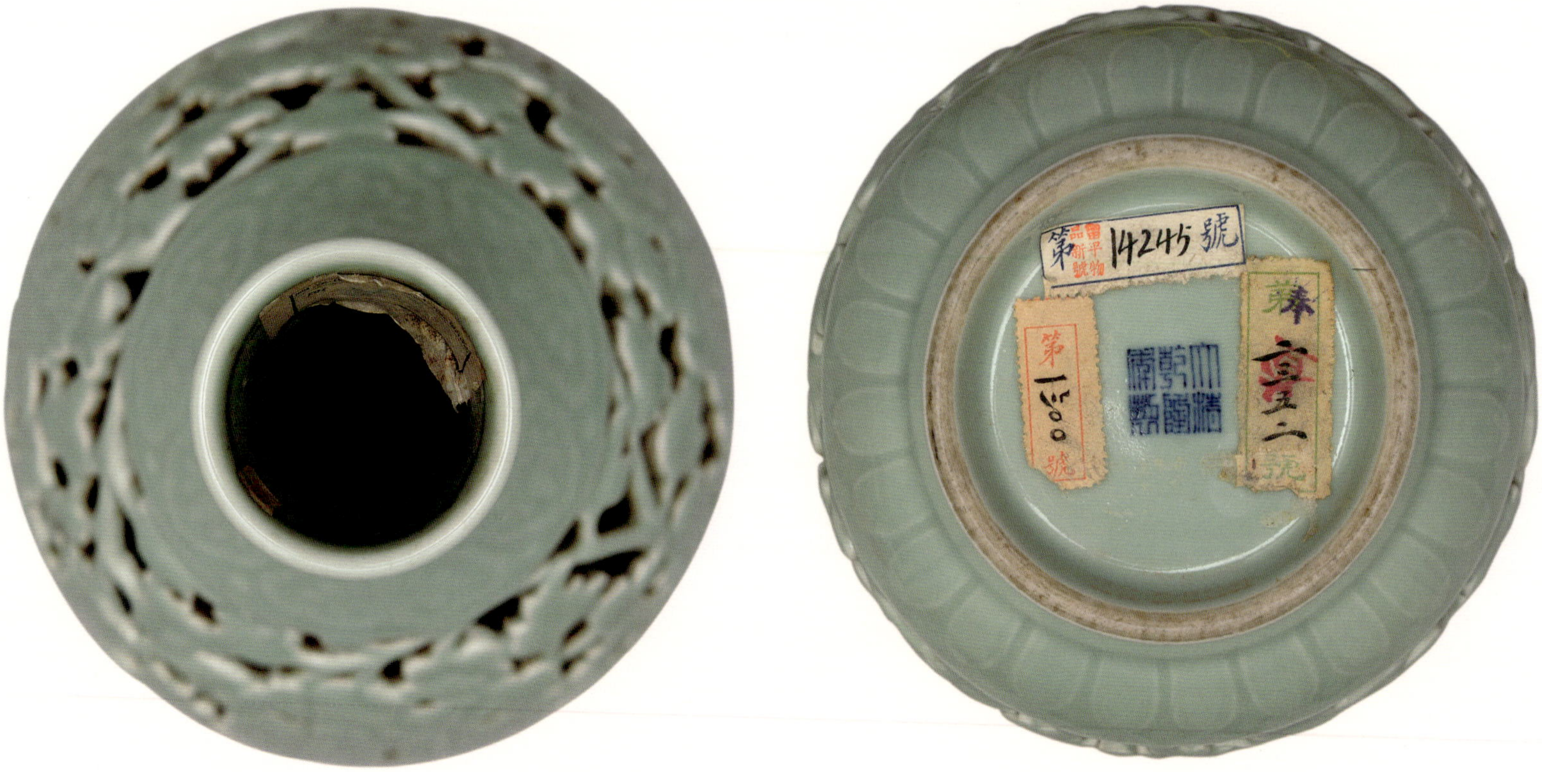

Jingdezhen kiln celadon openwork *yuhuchun* ('spring in a jade bottle') vase with peony scrolls design

Qianlong period, Qing dynasty, Height 32.5cm mouth diameter 5cm foot diameter 10cm, Collected by the Qing Palace, The Palace Museum

085 景德镇窑青釉葫芦瓶

清乾隆

通高 35.5 厘米　口径 3 厘米　足径 12.2 厘米

清宫旧藏

故宫博物院藏

瓶呈宝葫芦形，卧足。外壁施冬青釉，瓶内和圈足内均施透明釉。外底署青花篆体“大清乾隆年制”六字三行款。（陈润民）

Jingdezhen kiln celadon gourd-shaped vase

Qianlong period, Qing dynasty, Overall height 35.5cm mouth diameter 3cm foot diameter 12.2cm, Collected by the Qing Palace, The Palace Museum

086 景德镇窑青釉刻划缠枝花纹菱花口折腰碟

清乾隆

高 3 厘米　口径 8.5 厘米　足径 4 厘米

故宫博物院藏

碟外撇菱花口，浅弧壁，折腰，圈足。内、外和圈足内均施冬青釉。内外壁皆刻划缠枝花纹，近足处刻划仰莲瓣纹。足端无釉，露白色胎。内底署青花篆体“大清乾隆年制”六字双行款。在故宫博物院藏瓷中可见与此碟造型相同的明代宣德仿龙泉釉菱花口碟，此碟为清代乾隆朝景德镇御窑厂仿宣德朝产品。（蒋艺）

Jingdezhen kiln celadon saucer with bracket-lobed rim and angled wall and carved and incised floral scrolls design

Qianlong period, Qing dynasty, Height 3cm mouth diameter 8.5cm foot diameter 4cm, The Palace Museum

087 景德镇窑青釉刻划缠枝花纹菱花口折腰碟

清乾隆

高 3 厘米　口径 10.3 厘米　足径 6.5 厘米

清宫旧藏

故宫博物院藏

碟外撇菱花口，浅弧壁，折腰，圈足。内、外和圈足内均施青釉。足端无釉，露白色胎。内外壁皆刻划缠枝花纹，近足处刻划仰莲瓣纹。内底署青花篆体“大清乾隆年制”六字双行款。（蒋艺）

Jingdezhen kiln celadon saucer with bracket-lobed rim and angled wall and carved and incised floral scrolls design

Qianlong period, Qing dynasty, Height 3cm mouth diameter 10.3cm foot diameter 6.5cm, Collected by the Qing Palace, The Palace Museum

088 景德镇窑青釉钟式水丞

清

高 8.5 厘米　口径 1.5 厘米　足横 7.5 厘米　足纵 3 厘米

故宫博物院藏

水丞呈钟式，顶开小口，足外撇。通体施青釉。水丞前后两面模印诗句及纹饰，近顶处皆模印龙纹，下部一面模印“笔砚勤拈”四字，另一面模印“早攀仙桂”四字。足端不施釉，呈红褐色。（蒋艺）

Jingdezhen kiln celadon bell shaped water container

Qianlong period, Qing dynasty, Height 8.5cm mouth diameter1.5cm foot length 7.5cm foot width 3cm, The Palace Museum

089 景德镇窑青釉刻划缠枝花纹盘

清

高 5 厘米　口径 35 厘米　足径 17.8 厘米

清宫旧藏

故宫博物院藏

盘敞口，折沿，浅弧壁，圈足。内、外施青釉，釉色青翠，有较强玻璃质感。内底刻划缠枝花纹。圈足内无釉，露胎表面呈黄褐色。（孙悦）

Jingdezhen kiln celadon dish with carved and incised floral scrolls design

Qing dynasty, Height 5cm mouth diameter 35cm foot diameter 17.8cm, Collected by the Qing Palace, The Palace Museum

日本的仿龙泉青瓷

日本从 17 世纪开始仿烧龙泉青瓷，仿烧的历史虽短，但在世界各地仿龙泉青瓷中，其产品与龙泉窑产品相似度最高。从产品自身特点及装烧方法观察，日本烧造的仿龙泉青瓷是在中国龙泉青瓷以及越南仿烧龙泉青瓷技术的双重影响下而实现。具体而言，是以中国宋元龙泉窑名品为追求目标，采用越南钵场社窑的技术烧造而成。在早期仿品中，刮釉垫烧处有越南青瓷风格的深酱色护胎釉痕迹。

日本仿烧龙泉青瓷的窑场主要有三田窑、有田窑、万古窑、春日山窑等。产品中最著名的是锅岛青瓷和三田青瓷。窑具有垫圈、垫饼、支钉等，窑炉有分室龙窑、阶级窑和全倒焰式窑等。就窑炉技术来看，日本仿烧龙泉青瓷与当时日本自身的瓷器生产一起经历了由东方的传统技术向现代科技过渡的阶段。

Imitations of Longquan Celadon Fired in Japan

Japan started to imitate Longquan celadon in the 17th century. Despite the comparatively shorter history of copying, the Longquan style celadon fired in Japan are closest to real Longquan celadon compared with copies made in other countries. Based on observation of product characteristics and methods of setting in kiln, the Longquan style celadon copied in Japan had received influences from both the Longquan celadon of China and imitations of Longquan celadon from Vietnam. Specifically, the Japanese potters tried to reproduce prestigious vessels of Longquan celadon from the Song and Yuan periods, with the techniques from kilns of Bat Trang, Vietnam. In the early copies of Japan, the areas in base with glazes removed to avoid sticking with setters have brown-coloured washes (*hutaiyou* or 'body-protecting glaze' in Chinese), a feature known for Vietnam celadon.

Japanese kilns that copied Longquan celadon primarily include the kilns of Sanda, Arita, Banko, and Kasugayama. The most famous of these are celadon of Nabeshima and Sanda. Kiln furniture include ring-shaped setter, disc-shaped setter, and piece with protruding spikes for supporting vessels. Kiln types include multi-chambered dragon kilns, stepped kilns, and downdraft kilns. From the perspective of kiln technology, the Longquan style celadon fired in Japan also underwent a transformation from the oriental traditional techniques to modern science and technology, just like the contemporaneous porcelain production in Japan.

090 日本万古窑青釉刻缠枝花纹盖罐

日本江户时代天明年间

高 15.1 厘米　口径 12.7 厘米　足径 10.6 厘米

日本东京国立博物馆藏

本器模仿元代龙泉窑青釉罐，腹部刻缠枝花纹，腹下周圈饰莲花纹图案。底刻“天明年制万古”铭。当初用为执壶，所以附有器盖，与龙泉窑青瓷造型不同。

江户时代元文年间（1736 ~ 1741 年），桑名的富商沼波弄山在伊势（今三重县三重郡朝日町小向）开始烧造陶瓷器，最初烧制五彩器，天保二年（1831 年）以后也烧造粉彩等器物。在“万古烧”之中，不透明铜绿釉陶瓷被称为“万古青瓷”。（德留大辅）

Japanese celadon covered jar carved with floral scrolls design

Edo Era, Height 15.1cm mouth diameter 12.7cm foot diameter 10.6cm, The Tokyo National Museum, Japan

091 日本沙流川窑青釉刻弦纹盘残件

1630 ~ 1650 年

残高 4.6 厘米　残长 16.6 厘米　残宽 11.8 厘米

日本佐贺县立九州陶瓷文化馆藏

1610 年前后，受朝鲜烧制工艺影响，日本陶瓷制造业开始兴起，烧造中心为肥前国（今佐贺县与长崎市的绝大部分地区）有田地区。早期，染付瓷器（青花），即釉下钴蓝彩绘装饰，是这一地区的主要产品。但在 1630 年前后，青瓷的生产也很稳定。（日本佐贺县立九州陶瓷文化馆）

Fragment of Japanese Sarugawa kiln celadon dish carved with string design

1630-1650, Remaining height 4.6cm remaining length 16.6cm remaining width 11.8cm, The Kyushu Ceramic Museum of Saga Prefecture

092 日本沙流川窑青釉刻花卉纹花口盘残件

1630 ~ 1650 年

高 4.2 厘米　残长 24.5 厘米　残宽 15.4 厘米

日本佐贺县立九州陶瓷文化馆藏

盘花瓣口，浅腹，圈足，内壁一周刻条状装饰，盘心单线刻折枝花朵图案。满施青蓝色釉，釉面有开片，具有玻璃质感，局部釉层起泡、不平整，圈足足梢无釉。胎呈白灰色，泛黄，含杂质，外壁残存轮制痕迹。（冀洛源）

Fragment of Japanese Sarugawa kiln celadon dish with lobed rim and carved floral design

1630-1650, Height 4.2cm remaining length 24.5cm remaining width 15.4cm, The Kyushu Ceramic Museum of Saga Prefecture

093 日本沙流川窑青釉刻狮子牡丹纹洗残件

1630 ~ 1650 年

高 8.8 厘米　残长 17.8 厘米　残宽 15.4 厘米

日本佐贺县立九州陶瓷文化馆藏

洗唇口，曲腹，圈足，内底刻狮子牡丹图案。满施青绿色釉，微泛灰，具有玻璃质感，外底心无釉，存支烧痕。胎呈白灰色，泛黄，含杂质。（冀洛源）

Fragment of Japanese Sarugawa kiln celadon washer carved with design of lion and peony

1630-1650, Height 8.8cm remaining length 17.8cm remaining width 15.4cm, The Kyushu Ceramic Museum of Saga Prefecture

094 日本下白川窑青釉镂空三足盘残件

1660 ~ 1670 年

高 7.5 厘米　残长 22.6 厘米　残宽 12.2 厘米

日本佐贺县立九州陶瓷文化馆藏

盘底的釉以同心圆的方式刮除，并敷盖含铁黏土，以仿龙泉青瓷风格。器底留有肥前国称为“Chatsu 楪子”的盘形窑具痕迹，这表明了与中国相关的烧制技术此时已引入到本地陶瓷生产之中。（日本佐贺县立九州陶瓷文化馆）

Fragment of Japanese Shimoshirakawa kiln celadon tripod dish with design of openwork

1660-1670, Height 7.5cm remaining length 22.6cm remaining width 12.2cm, The Kyushu Ceramic Museum of Saga Prefecture

095 日本下白川窑青釉镂空三足盘残件

1660 ~ 1670 年

高 9 厘米　残长 23 厘米　残宽 14.2 厘米

日本佐贺县立九州陶瓷文化馆藏

盘折沿，直口，口沿下一周作整齐的镂空竖条纹装饰，折腹，浅圈足，圈足外均匀塑出三足，足作兽首状。内外壁满施青蓝色釉，釉面有开片，具有玻璃质感，胎呈灰白色，略疏松。外底圈足内一周为较宽的垫烧痕，露胎无釉，胎面呈深褐色。（冀洛源）

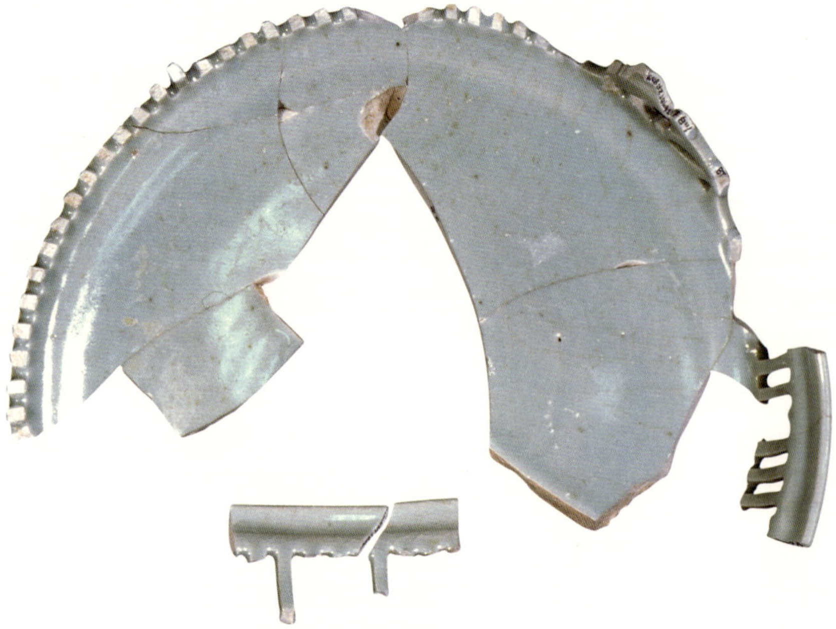

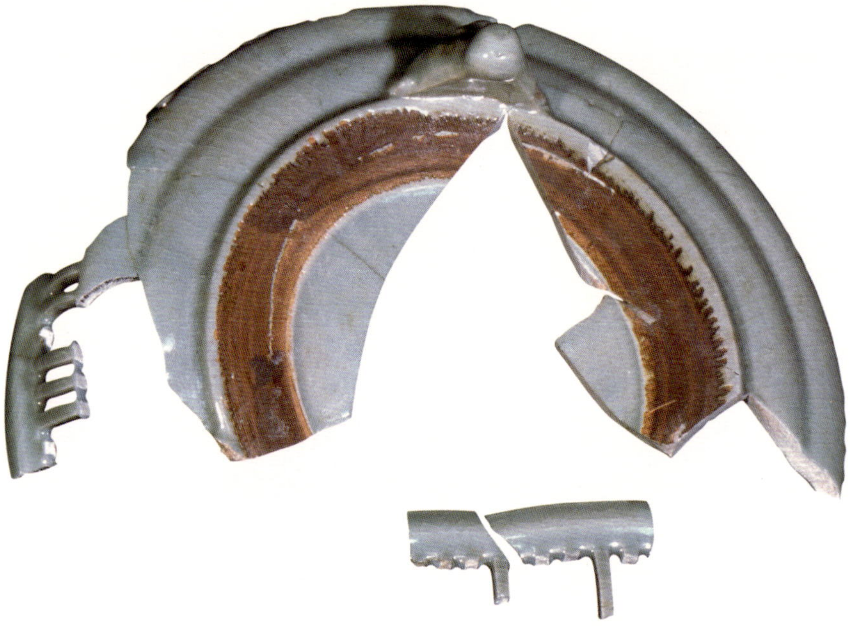

Fragment of Japanese Shimoshirakawa kiln celadon tripod dish with design of openwork

1660-1670, Height 9cm remaining length 23cm remaining width 14.2cm, The Kyushu Ceramic Museum of Saga Prefecture

096 日本下白川窑青釉镂空三足花口盘残件

1660 ~ 1670 年

残高 4.5 厘米　残长 15.3 厘米　残宽 12.8 厘米

日本佐贺县立九州陶瓷文化馆藏

盘花瓣口，口沿下一周作整齐的镂空六边形装饰，浅腹，浅圈足，原圈足外应均匀塑出三足。内外壁满施青蓝色釉，釉面有开片，具有玻璃质感，胎呈灰白色，略疏松。盘心残存支钉痕，外底圈足内一周为深褐色垫烧痕。（冀洛源）

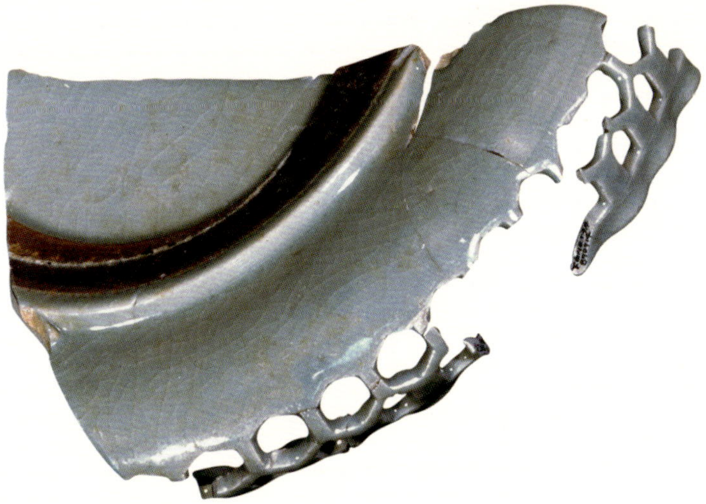

Fragment of Japanese Shimoshirakawa kiln celadon tripod dish with bracked-shaped and design of openwork

1660-1670, Remaining height 4.5cm remaining length 15.3cm remaining width 12.8cm, The Kyushu Ceramic Museum of Saga Prefecture

097 日本锅岛窑青釉印牡丹纹三足盘

日本江户时代早中期

高 8.5 厘米　口径 27.6 厘米　足径 17.7 厘米

日本东京国立博物馆藏

该器为江户时代（1603 ~ 1868 年）锅岛藩（今佐贺县及长崎县一部）藩窑所烧青瓷。“锅岛烧”虽以青花和五彩知名，但也生产出了高品质的青瓷产品。锅岛青瓷与景德镇窑青瓷一样，使用与白瓷相同的纯白瓷土，厚施青釉。锅岛青瓷的梳叶纹高圈足木杯形碟很有名，不过，也有像该器这样以三足替代圈足的器物，先以辘轳成型，再用印范印出浮雕状牡丹纹。（德留大辅）

Japanese celadon tripod dish impressed with peony design

Early and middle Edo Era, Height 8.5cm mouth diameter 27.6cm foot diameter 17.7cm, The Tokyo National Museum, Japan

098 日本青釉刻菊花纹花口盘

19 世纪

高 3.5 厘米　口径 25 厘米　足径 11 厘米

故宫博物院藏

盘花口，浅弧壁，圈足，足壁内敛。内、外施青釉，外底施酱釉，足端无釉。口沿一周刮釉，内底刻菊花纹，内壁刻划几何形，胎质细腻洁白。（张涵）

Japanese celadon dish with lobed rim and carved chrysanthemum design

19th Century, Height 3.5cm mouth diameter 25cm foot diameter 11cm, The Palace Museum

099 日本湖东窑青釉刻缠枝牡丹纹三足筒式炉

日本江户时代晚期（19 世纪）

高 7.7 厘米　口径 9.5 × 9.7 厘米

日本东京国立博物馆藏

炉身布满缠枝牡丹纹，外底露胎，有戳印“湖东”铭。

“湖东烧”始于文政十二年（1829 年），由彦根城下（今滋贺县彦根市）的旧衣商绢屋半兵卫等出资建造。此后，于 1842 年成为彦根藩的藩窑（官窑）。“湖东烧”窑场聘请濑户的陶工、“九谷烧”与“京烧”的画工等，又从当时先进的大窑场招聘优秀陶工，以生产高级产品为目标。19 世纪 50 年代，“湖东烧”迎来了黄金时代，这个时期以模仿中国明清时代陶瓷为主，也多见仿制日本“青手九谷”“肥前陶瓷”“濑户烧”的青花瓷产品。“湖东烧”青瓷以花瓶、盖托、香炉等与茶具相关的器形为主。（德留大辅）

Japanese celadon tripod incense burner carved with peony scrolls design

Late Edo Era, Height 7.7cm mouth diameter 9.5×9.7cm, The Tokyo National Museum, Japan

附 5 龙泉窑青釉刻折枝花纹三足筒式炉

明早中期

高 18 厘米 口径 24.5 厘米 足距 17 厘米

清宫旧藏

故宫博物院藏

炉敞口，方唇，上宽下窄筒形腹，平底，底下承以三足。内、外施青釉，釉面光润。外壁上下凸弦纹之间刻折枝花纹。外底有一圈刮釉露胎，系垫圈垫烧处。（高晓然）

Longquan celadon cylindrical tripod incense burner carved with floral spray design

Early to middle Ming dynasty, Height 18cm mouth diameter 24.5cm distance between feet 17cm, Collected by the Qing Palace, The Palace Museum

100 日本三田窑青釉镂空螭龙纹香炉

日本江户时代晚期（19世纪）
高5.5厘米　径7×6.6厘米
日本东京国立博物馆藏

炉身镂空螭龙纹及卷草纹，制作精巧，外底有“钦古”刻铭。器形仿自中国元代香炉，在日本被称为“天龙寺手”。

本器为兵库县三田市所烧青瓷。“三田烧”创始于江户时代宝历年间（1751～1764年），青瓷的烧造一般认为始于18世纪前后，其鼎盛期是文化年间（1804～1818年）至天保（1830～1844年）初期，从京都聘请名工钦古堂龟佑（1765～1837年）进行指导。其所烧青瓷器被称作三田青瓷，最为著名。（德留大辅）

Japanese celadon incense burner with openwork *chi* dragon design
Late Edo Era, Height 5.5cm diameter 7×6.6cm, The Tokyo National Museum, Japan

101 青釉镂空亭式灯

约 19 世纪

高 30.5 厘米　宽 27 厘米　深 25 厘米

英国杜伦大学东方博物馆藏

灯为少见的六角形凉亭造型，六角攒尖屋顶，六面微凹，六脊角部塑出角兽，顶部作莲花苞状宝珠，珠座位置留有穿绳的孔洞，以便悬挂。灯身六面均刻出自上而下的额枋、格子窗、花卉纹钩栏三部分。灯座六足，足作垂莲叶状，座内有一圆孔，可放灯烛。该灯通体施青绿色釉，唯六足足梢及外底中心无釉露胎。(Rachel Barclay)

＊此灯的产地有争议，有日本产和中国龙泉产两种观点。

Celadon pavilion-shaped lamp in openwork

Ca. 19th Century, Height 30.5cm width 27cm depth 25cm, The Oriental Museum, Durham University, Britain

102 日本青釉刻缠枝牡丹纹双环耳瓶

1912 年

高 35.8 厘米　口径 7.9 厘米　足径 11.5 厘米

日本宫川香山制

日本东京国立博物馆藏

瓶颈部至口部直立，颈下部略带弧线，形制端正。器身饰以大花瓣牡丹纹和缠枝纹，雕刻精巧，釉色艳丽。器物烧造于大正元年（1912 年），是为纪念大正天皇即位而献给帝室博物馆（今东京国立博物馆）的作品之一。

在日本陶艺史上，明治时代（1868 ~ 1912 年）至大正时代（1912 ~ 1926 年）是从工匠到陶艺家的过渡时期。第一代宫川香山（Miyagawa Kozan）（1842 ~ 1916 年）是其中的代表人物之一，活跃在日本国内外的博览会上，被任命为帝室技艺员。宫川出生于京都的制陶世家，自幼喜欢陶瓷。19 岁继承祖业，开始烧造以茶具为主的陶瓷器。明治 4 年（1871 年），为了生产出口陶瓷，在横滨的横山建造窑场，号称真葛窑。从这里出口的陶瓷器也被称为“Makuzu ware”，在海外知名度很高。创业当初，多仿制在欧美各国颇受欢迎的“萨摩烧”的“金襕手”（描金）器物，此后转向瓷器烧造，关注欧美的流行动态，遵照中国清代陶瓷的制作规范，烧造青花或青瓷等器物。（德留大辅）

Japanese celadon vase with two handles and carved peony scrolls design

1912, Height 35.8cm mouth diameter 7.9cm foot diameter 11.5cm, Made by Miyagawa Kozan, The Tokyo National Museum, Japan

103 日本青釉凤耳盘口瓶

1914 年 12 月
高 24.1 厘米　口径 9.9 厘米　足径 8.8 厘米
日本诹访苏山制
日本东京国立博物馆藏

器物仿南宋龙泉窑青釉凤耳瓶。不仅日本镰仓时代的遗迹出土过同样的凤耳瓶，而且历史上也被著名的大名家所收藏。至今有很多南宋至元代的龙泉青瓷流传下来，其中不少被指定为日本的国宝或重要文化财。这类器物是日本人所憧憬的青瓷之一，对近现代陶艺家影响至深。

与第一代宫川香山一样，诹访苏山（Suwa Sozan）也是明治、大正时代的代表陶工之一。他出生于今石川县金泽，22 岁时来到东京学习陶画，不久回到家乡，供职于九谷陶器公司。此后，任石川县立工业学校雕刻科的助教，承担“九谷烧”的陶瓷雕刻。明治 33 年（1900 年）受聘于京都锦光山制陶所，1940 年独立经营，在京都五条坂开窑，烧造青瓷。所烧器物精美，被称为“苏山青瓷”。大正 6 年（1917 年）被任命为帝室技艺员。

Japanese celadon mallet vase with dish mouth and phoenix-head handles
1914, Height 24.1cm mouth diameter 9.9cm bottom diameter 8.8cm, Made by Suwa Sozan, The Tokyo National Museum, Japan

附 6 龙泉窑青釉凤耳盘口瓶

南宋

高 27 厘米　口径 9.8 厘米　足径 10.2 厘米

松阳县博物馆藏

瓶浅盘口，筒形长颈，斜折肩，筒腹，圈足。筒形长颈两侧对称置凤耳。胎白，细腻坚硬。通体施粉青色釉，釉层较厚，状若凝脂，晶莹如玉，足端无釉。造型规整优美，胎质细腻精良，粉青釉层凝厚如玉，是龙泉窑青瓷中的稀有珍品。

此类长颈瓶在汝窑、南宋官窑中多有发现，然以凤或鱼作两耳者，仅见于龙泉窑产品中。（刘鼎）

Longquan celadon mallet vase with dish mouth and phoenix-head handles

Southern Song dynasty, Height 27cm mouth diameter 9.8cm foot diameter 10.2cm, The Songyang County Museum

越南的仿龙泉青瓷

越南烧造仿龙泉青瓷的窑场主要分布于越南北部，其中舟逗窑和钵场社窑是当地历史上的两大陶瓷生产中心。

越南烧造的仿龙泉青瓷常见折沿盘、敞口碗、瓜棱执壶、钵、渣斗、小罐等。其青釉发色青中泛黄，器底有刻意模仿龙泉青瓷外底“火石红”的痕迹。装饰技法采用与龙泉青瓷相似的刻划花技法，纹饰也多模仿同时期或稍早的龙泉青瓷。越南窑场烧造仿龙泉青瓷的窑炉多为龙窑，窑具常见匣钵、垫圈、垫饼等，与龙泉窑所用窑具相近。其中也有部分碗、盘采用涩圈叠烧法烧成，精品则模仿龙泉青瓷的刮釉垫烧工艺。

Imitations of Longquan Celadon Fired in Vietnam

The kilns that fired Longquan style celadon in Vietnam are mainly located in the north of the country. Among these, Chu Dau and Bat Trang are the two major ceramic centres in history. The common Longquan style celadon fired in Vietnam include dishes with everted rim, bowls with wide opening, ewers of melon form, deep bowls, jars for slops, jarlets, etc. Their celadon glaze appears green with a yellow tinge, and on the bottom is the *huoshihong* or 'burnt stone red' that is typical for Longquan celadon, which indicates intentional imitating. The decorative techniques of carving or incising used for such Vietname wares are similar to Longquan celadon, and decorative motifs also often imitate those of contemporaneous or slightly earlier Longquan products. The kilns that fired copies of Longquan celadon are usually dragon kilns, and the kiln furniture is close to that of Longquan, including common pieces such as saggar, ring-shaped setter, and disc-shaped setter. Some of the bowls and dishes are stacked for firing in kiln, with an unglazed ring on the inside to avoid sticking with each other. Finer pieces are fully glazed and then have the glaze removed at part of the bottom to avoid sticking with setters in firing, just like the Longquan celadon.

104 越南青釉瓜棱形双系盖罐

14 ~ 15 世纪

通高 8.5 厘米　口径 4.9 厘米　底径 6.8 厘米

香港中文大学文物馆藏

盖罐作瓜棱状，扁圆腹，平底无釉。灰白胎，施青釉，釉面满布细碎裂纹。罐身作六瓣瓜棱形，两肩塑贴拱形小系。底部变形开裂，实用性受损。罐盖作穹窿形，盖顶塑贴拱形钮，内壁无釉。（王冠宇）

Vietnamese celadon melon-shaped covered jar

14-15th Century, Overall height 8.5cm mouth diameter 4.9cm bottom diameter 6.8cm, The Art Museum, the Chinese University of Hong Kong

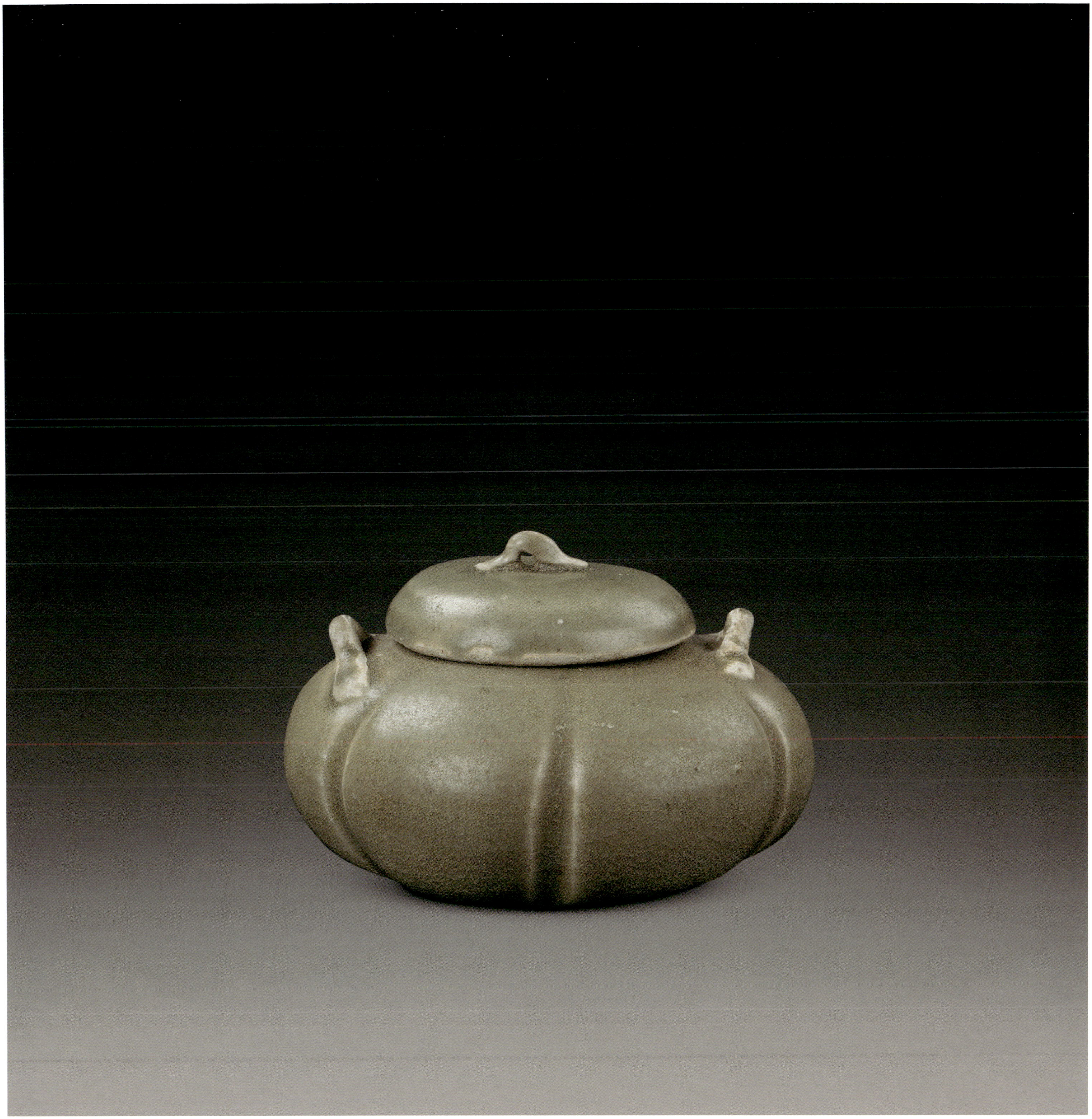

105 越南青釉瓜棱形小罐

14 ~ 15 世纪

高 6.5 厘米　口径 2.5 厘米　足径 3.8 厘米

香港中文大学文物馆藏

罐直口，短颈，圆鼓腹，腹作瓜棱状，圈足。胎色灰黄，施青绿釉，釉层较薄，施釉不均匀，足部无釉。（王冠宇）

Vietnamese celadon melon-shaped jar

14-15th Century, Height 6.5cm mouth diameter 2.5cm foot diameter 3.8cm, The Art Museum, the Chinese University of Hong Kong

106 越南青釉瓜棱形小罐

14～15世纪

高4.8厘米　口径1.7厘米　足径2.7厘米

香港中文大学文物馆藏

罐体小巧，作瓜棱形。小口，短颈，圆腹，圈足。灰白胎，内、外施青绿釉，釉层较薄，釉面开裂。器腹作六瓣瓜棱形，肩部塑贴两个花形小钮。（王冠宇）

Vietnamese celadon melon-shaped jar

14-15th Century, Height 4.8cm mouth diameter 1.7cm foot diameter 2.7cm, The Art Museum, the Chinese University of Hong Kong

107 越南青釉钵

14 ~ 15 世纪

高 16.6 厘米　口径 18 厘米　足径 6.5 厘米

香港中文大学文物馆藏

钵口微敛，圆鼓腹，圈足微外撇，足部无釉。灰黄胎，胎体厚重，内、外施灰青釉。外口沿下饰二道凹弦纹，腹部垂直刮出竖条纹。内壁可见拉坯痕，内底见五枚细小支钉痕，为叠、套烧工艺痕迹。（王冠宇）

Vietnamese celadon earthen bowl

14-15th Century, Height 16.6cm mouth diameter 18cm foot diameter 6.5cm, The Art Museum, the Chinese University of Hong Kong

108 越南青釉刻弦纹钵

14 ~ 15 世纪

高 10.4 厘米　口径 13 厘米　足径 5 厘米

香港中文大学文物馆藏

钵直口，深腹微鼓，折底，圈足。灰白胎，内、外施青黄色釉，外壁施釉未及底。外口沿下及腹近底处均刻凹弦纹二道。钵内底涩圈，有叠烧痕。圈足未施釉，足端粘釉，应为叠烧所致。（王冠宇）

Vietnamese celadon earthen bowl carved with string design

14-15th Century, Height 10.4cm mouth diameter 13cm foot diameter 5cm, The Art Museum, the Chinese University of Hong Kong

泰国的仿龙泉青瓷

泰国仿烧龙泉青瓷的窑场主要有素可太府的西萨查那莱窑、清迈府的山甘烹窑、帕尧府的旺布阿窑、“旺”河（Wang River）流域的旺努阿窑以及清莱府的攀窑等。泰国烧造的仿龙泉青瓷以折沿盘、碗、盖罐、双系小罐等最为常见，胎釉质量均较差，青釉玻璃质感较强且发色不一。装饰上多见模仿龙泉窑瓷器上的鱼纹、花卉纹、菊瓣纹、莲瓣纹等。

在今越南、马来西亚、文莱、菲律宾、印度尼西亚等地的沉船中均曾发现泰国烧造的仿龙泉青瓷，可见这类瓷器是当时泰国重要的外销瓷品种，反映出当时世界各地对龙泉青瓷的旺盛需求，也说明泰国的制瓷业深受以龙泉窑为代表的中国制瓷业影响。

Imitations of Longquan Celadon Fired in Thailand

The kilns that fired Longquan style celadon in Thailand mainly include the Si Satchanalai kilns in Sukhothai province, the San Kamphaeng kilns in Chiang Mai province, the Wang Bua kilns in Phayao Province, the Phan kilns in Chiang Rai province, and the Wang Nua kilns of Wang River (adjacent to Chiang Rai). The most common vessels fired in Thailand in imitation of Longquan celadon are dishes with everted mouth rims, bowls, lidded jars, and jarlets with double lugs. Their body material and glaze is inferior in quality, and the celadon glaze is glassy and vary in tones. The designs usually imitate those of Longquan celadon, including fish, flowers, chrysanthemum petals, lotus petals, etc.

Imitations of Longquan celadon from Thailand have been discovered in shipwrecks found in waters of Vietnam, Malaysia, Brunei, the Philippines, Indonesia, etc. These demonstrate that the Longquan style celadon were important export ceramics of Thailand, and there was a great demand for Longquan celadon from many parts of the world, while ceramic industry in Thailand had been deeply influenced by Chinese ceramics represented by Longquan celadon.

109 泰国青釉刻菊瓣纹双系罐

10 ~ 13 世纪

高 12.7 厘米　口径 3.4 厘米　足径 8 厘米

故宫博物院藏

罐唇口，短颈，鼓腹，圈足。颈、肩之间对称置圆环形系。通体施青釉，釉不及底，釉层清亮，玻璃质感较强，釉面布满开片。肩部刻菊瓣纹。（赵聪月）

Thai celadon jar with two handles and carved chrysanthemum petals design

10-13th Century, Height 12.7cm mouth diameter 3.4cm foot diameter 8cm, The Palace Museum

110 泰国青釉刻菊瓣纹双系罐

10 ~ 13 世纪

高 15 厘米　口径 4.5 厘米　足径 8.8 厘米

故宫博物院藏

罐唇口，短颈，鼓腹，圈足。颈、肩之间对称置圆环形系。通体施青釉，釉不及底，釉面布满开片，底部有积釉。肩、腹相接处凸起一道弦纹，肩部和腹下部均刻菊瓣纹。（赵聪月）

Thai celadon jar with two handles and carved chrysanthemum petals design

10-13th Century, Height 15cm mouth diameter 4.5cm foot diameter 8.8cm, The Palace Museum

附 7　龙泉窑青釉印缠枝牡丹纹双系罐

元

高 10 厘米　口径 4.6 厘米　足径 5 厘米

故宫博物院藏

罐圆唇，短颈，鼓腹，圈足。肩部对称置圆环系。通体施青釉，釉色泛黄。腹中部凸起一道弦纹将腹分为上下两部分，上部饰四组花卉纹，下部饰仰莲瓣纹。底部无釉。（赵聪月）

Longquan celadon jar with two handles and impressed design of peony scrolls

Yuan dynasty, Height 10cm mouth diameter 4.6cm foot diameter 5cm, The Palace Museum

附 8　龙泉窑青釉褐斑印龙纹双系罐

元

高 7 厘米　口径 3 厘米　足径 3 厘米

故宫博物院藏

罐圆唇，短束颈，丰肩，鼓腹，腹下渐收敛，矮圈足。颈、肩之间对称置圆环系。内、外均施青釉，有开片，外壁涂点褐斑。上腹部饰盘龙纹，下腹部饰卷云纹，近底处饰海水纹。足部无釉，露胎呈火石红色。（陈志鸿）

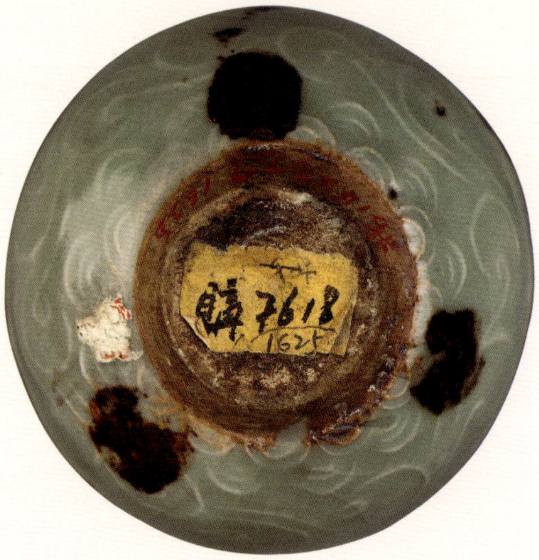

Longquan celadon jar with two handles, iron-brown splashes and impressed dragon design

Yuan dynasty, Height 7cm mouth diameter 3cm foot diameter 3cm, The Palace Museum

附 9　龙泉窑青釉印菊花纹双系罐

元

高 7.8 厘米　口径 3.8 厘米　足径 4.9 厘米

平潭大练岛沉船出土

中国国家博物馆藏

罐直口，短颈，鼓腹，饼形实足。颈两侧对称置圆环形系。釉呈青绿色，釉色不均，釉面布满开片，局部釉面呈青褐、黄褐色。器表釉层较厚，纹样模糊不清。

大练岛元代沉船位于福建省平潭县大练岛与小练岛之间海域，2006 年发现，出水遗物绝大部分为陶瓷器，以青瓷为主，釉色以青绿为主，此外还有青黄、青褐、青灰等色，有的颜色深浅不一。该船出水的这批青瓷制作精美，是典型的元代龙泉窑产品。

元代龙泉窑无论烧造工艺还是装饰，在南宋的基础上都有了较大改变，主要体现在胎体厚重、造型更显古朴。（申沉）

Longquan celadon jar with two handles and impressed chrysanthemum design

Yuan dynasty, Height 7.8cm mouth diameter 3.8cm foot diameter 4.9cm, From the shipwreck at Dalian island, Pingtan, The National Museum of China

111 泰国西萨查那莱窑青釉刻几何纹洗

14 世纪

高 5.1 厘米　口径 21.5 厘米

英国维多利亚与艾伯特博物馆藏

洗内施青釉，刻几何纹，外壁无釉。口镶有金属釦。（英国维多利亚与艾伯特博物馆）

Thai Si Satchanalai kiln celadon washer carved with geometric design

14th Century, Height 5.1cm mouth diameter 21.5cm, The Victoria and Albert Museum, Britain

112 泰国西萨查那莱窑青釉刻弦纹双系罐

15 世纪

高 17.4 厘米　径 17.8 厘米

英国维多利亚与艾伯特博物馆藏

历史上，浙江出产的青瓷曾广泛出口至菲律宾、印度尼西亚和东南亚大陆。当地制陶工人对龙泉青瓷加以模仿，到 1300 年，泰国和越南已成功发展出自己的“青瓷”产业。1400 年以后，位于泰国中北部的西萨查那莱生产的绿釉和棕色釉瓷占据了东南亚出口市场的主流。（英国维多利亚与艾伯特博物馆）

Thai Si Satchanalai kiln celadon jar with two handles and carved string design

15th Century, Height 17.4cm diameter 17.8cm, The Victoria and Albert Museum, Britain

113 泰国西萨查那莱窑青釉刻划牡丹纹菱花口折沿盘

15 ~ 16 世纪
高 9 厘米　口径 29 厘米
海伦与约翰·埃斯皮尔为纪念帕特里克·沃尔克捐赠
英国维多利亚与艾伯特博物馆藏

盘菱花口，折沿，内外施青釉。盘内刻划花装饰，内底刻五瓣花，内壁刻四朵牡丹花。足内凹，足外侧有管状支架留下的痕迹和竖条纹装饰。（英国维多利亚与艾伯特博物馆）

Thai Si Satchanalai kiln celadon dish with everted rim and carved and incised peony design
15-16th Century, Height 9cm mouth diameter 29cm, Given by Helen and John Espir in memory of Patrick Walker, The Victoria and Albert Museum, Britain

114 泰国宋加洛窑青釉刻竖条纹杯

14 ~ 15 世纪

高 4.6 厘米　口径 4 厘米　足径 3.1 厘米

香港中文大学文物馆藏

杯体小巧，直口微敛，腹微外鼓，圈足微外撇。灰白胎，内、外施青釉，外壁施釉不及底。外口沿下刻弦纹数道，腹部刮出竖条纹。假圈足，平底未挖足。（王冠宇）

Thai Sangkhalok kiln celadon cup carved with string design

14-15th Century, Height 4.6cm mouth diameter 4cm foot diameter 3.1cm, The Art Museum, the Chinese University of Hong Kong

115 泰国宋加洛窑青釉刻划莲瓣纹双系罐

14 ~ 16 世纪
高 14.7 厘米
D. R. 海 · 尼夫捐赠
英国大英博物馆藏

炻瓷。罐唇口，短颈，鼓腹，圈足。颈部与肩部之间对称置双系。通体施青釉，釉面布满开片。肩、腹部相接处有弦纹三道，肩部有刻划莲瓣纹。（孙悦）

Thai Sangkhalok kiln celadon jar with two handles and carved and incised lotus petals design
14-16th Century, Height 14.7cm, Given by D.R.Hay-Neef, The British Museum, Britain

116 泰国宋加洛窑青釉刻划菊瓣纹碗

14 ~ 16 世纪

高 6.5 厘米　口径 10.5 厘米

D. R. 海 · 尼夫捐赠

英国大英博物馆藏

炻瓷。碗唇口，弧壁，圈足。通体施青釉，底足一周施釉不均，有无釉处露出素胎。碗通体有细碎开片，外壁一周刻划菊瓣纹。（孙悦）

Thai Sangkhalok kiln celadon bowl with carved and incised chrysanthemum petals design

14-16th Century, Height 14.7cm mouth diameter 10.5cm, Given by D.R.Hay-Neef, The British Museum, Britain

117 泰国宋加洛窑青釉刻莲花纹折沿盘

14 ~ 16 世纪

口径 25.8 厘米

英国大英博物馆藏

盘中部刻有莲花图案，花瓣沿凹弧壁延伸。青釉汇集在刻花处，形成美观的装饰效果。外侧部分施釉，厚釉沿盘身垂流，盘身经烧成后氧化成橘红色。（英国大英博物馆）

Thai Sangkhalok kiln celadon dish with everted rim and carved lotus design

14-16th Century, Mouth diameter 25.8cm, The British Museum, Britain

缅甸的仿龙泉青瓷

缅甸地区仿烧龙泉窑青瓷的窑场，主要分布于仰光北部的拉固北（Lagumbyee）地区和西南部的卑谬（Phayagyi）、考穆（Kawmn）地区。卑谬窑炉剖面大体呈椭圆形，与泰国西萨查那莱窑类似，均为馒头窑。该窑主要烧造碗、盘类瓷器，釉色以青绿为主，在器物造型上多模仿龙泉青瓷。窑址附近发现有筒状、柱状支烧窑具。

Imitations of Longquan Celadon Fired in Burma

The kilns that fired Longquan style celadon in Burma are mainly located in Lagumbyee north of Rangoon, as well as Phayagyi and Kawmn in the southwest. The kilns of Phayagyi are roughly oval in section and are all *mantou* (lit. steamed bun) kilns, similar to the Si Satchanalai kilns in Sukhothai, Thailand. The primary vessel types fired at the Phayagyi kilns are bowls and dishes, which appear green with blue tinge in glaze colour, and imitate the shapes of Longquan celadon. Kiln site finds include kiln furniture that is shaped like barrels or columns used for supporting vessels in firing.

118 缅甸青釉碗残件

15 ~ 16 世纪

残长 9.8 厘米　残宽 9.3 厘米

阿联酋拉斯海马酋长国国家博物馆藏

碗直壁，圈足。圈足、外底无釉。釉色青翠，玻璃质感强，碗心积釉出呈墨绿色。内、外壁光素无装饰。（翟毅）

Fragment of Burmese celadon bowl

15-16th Century, Remaining length 9.8cm remaining width 9.3cm, The National Museum of Ras Al Khaimah, UAE

119 缅甸青釉盘残件

15 ~ 16 世纪

残长 13.1 厘米　残宽 10.9 厘米

阿联酋拉斯海马酋长国国家博物馆藏

盘弧壁，浅圈足。通体施青釉，釉色青灰，外底有刮釉痕迹。内壁刻弦纹、竖条纹。残片可见 3 处贯穿器壁的焗孔。（翟毅）

Fragment of Burmese celadon dish

15-16th Century, Remaining length 13.1cm remaining width 10.9cm, The National Museum of Ras Al Khaimah, UAE

120 缅甸青釉盘残件

15 ~ 16 世纪

残长 13.2 厘米　残宽 10.2 厘米

阿联酋拉斯海马酋长国国家博物馆藏

盘微弧腹，浅圈足。青釉泛灰蓝色。足端釉面磨损，外底刮釉。胎体略疏松，呈浅褐色。（翟毅）

Fragment of Burmese celadon dish

15-16th Century, Remaining length 13.2cm remaining width 10.2cm, The National Museum of Ras Al Khaimah, UAE

121 缅甸青釉盘残件

15～16世纪

残长7.8厘米 残宽7.2厘米

阿联酋拉斯海马酋长国国家博物馆藏月

盘微弧腹，浅圈足。青釉泛灰蓝色。足端釉面磨损，外底刮釉。胎体略疏松，呈浅褐色。（翟毅）

Fragment of Burmese celadon dish

15-16th Century, Remaining length 7.8cm remaining width 7.2cm, The National Museum of Ras Al Khaimah, UAE

122 缅甸青釉刻划卷草纹折沿盘残件

15 ~ 16 世纪

高 8.2 厘米　口径 40 厘米　足径 19 厘米

阿联酋拉斯海马酋长国国家博物馆藏

盘敞口，折沿，边缘略卷，弧腹，圈足。通体施釉，釉色青翠，透明度强，积釉处呈墨绿色。盘底圈足内侧不施釉，呈现火石红色。盘内壁刻划卷草纹，折沿处刻划菊瓣纹。

缅甸的青瓷窑业目前发现集中在下缅甸的伊洛瓦底江三角洲，例如仰光省的瑞迪（Twant）地区，勃固省的卑谬（Phayagyi）等地区。其中大量盘、碗类青瓷模仿龙泉窑青瓷产品，在 15 世纪之后大量销往海外。在波斯湾阿联酋祖尔法（Julfar）遗址大量发现这类仿龙泉窑青瓷与龙泉青瓷产品混杂在一起。（翟毅）

Fragment of Burmese celadon dish with everted rim and carved and incised grass design

15-16th Century, Height 8.2cm mouth diameter 40cm foot diameter 19cm, The National Museum of Ras Al Khaimah, UAE

埃及、叙利亚、伊朗地区的仿龙泉青瓷

埃及、叙利亚、伊朗地区烧造的仿龙泉青瓷窑器属于陶器，出现于 13 ~ 14 世纪。当地陶工采用西亚、北非地区传统釉陶的釉色、器形、装饰，烧造仿龙泉窑青釉陶器。产品釉色有当地流行的孔雀蓝或孔雀绿釉，也有直接仿烧龙泉窑青釉者。仿烧龙泉窑的器物以盘、碗为主，大盘的口沿模仿龙泉窑瓷器凸起边缘，盘、碗的腹部多装饰菊瓣纹，盘内底模仿龙泉窑青瓷的模印贴花双鱼。从垫烧痕迹来看，还有模仿龙泉青瓷足底刮釉的做法。

就目前所知，埃及、叙利亚、伊朗等国烧造龙泉窑青瓷风格釉陶的中心窑场分布于埃及福斯塔特（Fustat），伊朗卡尚（Kashan）、大不里士（Tabris）、塔诃特苏莱曼（Takhte Soleymān）、苏丹尼耶（Soltaniyeh），叙利亚大马士革（Damas）、巴里斯 - 麦斯肯内（Balis Meskene）等地。

Imitations of Longquan Celadon Fired in Egypt, Syria and Iran

The ceramics made in Egypt, Syria and Iran to copy Longquan celadon are pottery in terms of body material. Local potters applied the glaze colour, vessel form and decoration of traditional glazed pottery in West Asia and North Africa in their attempt to copy Longquan celadon. The glaze include both turquoise glaze of blue or green colour popular in local regions, and also direct imitation of the celadon glaze of Longquan wares. The vessels copying Longquan celadon are primarily dishes and bowls. Large dishes imitate Longquan celadon in the protruding edges of mouth rims, while dishes and bowls are often decorated with chrysanthemum petals on their bodies. On the inside of pottery dishes are imitation of sprig-moulded double-fish design that are commonly applied to Longquan celadon dishes. Judging from traces of kiln firing left on the bottom of vessels, the potters also copied the Longquan technique of removing parts of the glaze on the bottom for setting.

The kilns that had fired pottery in style of Longquan celadon are situated in Fustat (old Cairo), Egypt; Kashan, Tabris, Takhte Soleymān, and Soltaniyeh in Iran; and Damas and Balis Meskene in Syria, as known to date.

123 埃及青釉灯

13 ~ 14 世纪
高 4.2 厘米　宽 9.5 厘米　厚 9 厘米
约翰 · F. 拉姆斯登爵士捐赠
英国维多利亚与艾伯特博物馆藏

灰色扁碗形陶灯，边沿内收呈唇形，有一小环柄，通身施青釉。（英国维多利亚与艾伯特博物馆）

Egyptian celadon lamp
13-14th Century, Height 4.2cm width 9.5cm thickness 9cm, Given by Sir John F. Ramsden, Bart., The Victoria and Albert Museum, Britain

124 埃及青釉十系罐残件

14 世纪

高 9.5 厘米　口径 10.8 厘米

英国大英博物馆藏

球根状花瓶，为陶器，施仿青釉。出自埃及尼罗河三角洲开罗福斯塔特地区。

Fragment of Egyptian celadon jar with ten handles

14th Century, Height 9.5cm mouth diameter 10.8cm, The British Museum, Britain

125 埃及灰绿釉模印贴花鱼纹碗残件

14 世纪

残高 8 厘米　残厚 3.1 厘米　残宽 11.3 厘米

埃及开罗古城出土

G. D. 霍恩布洛尔阁下捐赠

英国维多利亚与艾伯特博物馆藏

陶片为一带圈足浅陶碗的中间部分。碎片中心有一浮雕状鱼。通体施绿松石色釉。系仿龙泉青瓷作品。

Fragment of Egyptian grayish celadon bowl impressed with twin fish design

14th Century, Remaining height 8cm remaining width11.3cm remaining thickness 3.1cm, Excavated from Old Cairo, Given by G. D. Hornblower esq. G.D.,
The Victoria and Albert Museum, Britain

附 10 龙泉窑青釉模印贴花双鱼纹折沿洗

元

高 3.5 厘米　口径 12.8 厘米　足径 6 厘米

故宫博物院藏

洗敞口，平折沿，浅弧腹，圈足。盘内、外和圈足内均施青釉，外底有一涩圈无釉，中心留有一小撮釉。内底塑贴双鱼，外壁刻莲瓣纹。（唐雪梅）

Longquan celadon washer with everted rim and impressed twin fish design

Yuan dynasty, Height 3.5cm mouth diameter 12.8cm foot diameter 6cm, The Palace Museum

126 埃及孔雀蓝釉印三鱼纹折沿盘

14 世纪
高 5 厘米　口径 23 厘米
英国大英博物馆藏

中东以仿制中国青花瓷器而著称，但这些进口国同样以本地原料仿制龙泉青瓷。由于烧成温度较中国瓷器低，致使此陶盘硬度不及中国龙泉青瓷。（英国大英博物馆）

Egyptian peacock blue glazed dish with everted rim and impressed three fish design
14th Century, Height 5cm mouth diameter 23cm, The British Museum, Britain

127 伊朗青釉印鱼纹高足敛口碗

12 ~ 13 世纪
高 7.6 厘米　口径 14.3 厘米
英国维多利亚与艾伯特博物馆藏

此高足敛口碗属于伊朗用低温釉模仿龙泉青瓷的陶制品。内底中心模印鱼纹，外沿刻有阿拉伯文。（英国维多利亚与艾伯特博物馆）

Iranian celadon bowl with high stem and impressed fish design
12-13th Century, Height 7.6cm mouth diameter 14.3cm, The Victoria and Albert Museum, Britain

附11 龙泉窑青釉刻莲瓣纹敛口碗

南宋

高 6 厘米　口径 14 厘米　足径 4.4 厘米

故宫博物院藏

碗敛口，窄折肩，斜曲腹，圈足，满施青绿釉。碗心划单弦纹，内印一朵折枝牡丹。外壁一周刻仰莲瓣纹，刻工流畅、干练。圈足平削，足梢无釉，露胎，胎面呈焦黄色。（冀洛源）

Longquan celadon bowl carved with lotus petals design

Southern Song dynasty, Height 6cm, mouth diameter 14cm, foot diameter 4.4cm, The Palace Museum

128 伊朗绿釉印四鱼纹折沿盘

15 ~ 16 世纪

高 6.8 厘米　口径 34.7 厘米

弗兰克 · 布兰格温爵士捐赠

英国维多利亚与艾伯特博物馆藏

这只伊朗制造的盘子在造型、装饰和颜色上均受到中国青瓷的启发。出自中国南方龙泉的青瓷器是 14 ~ 15 世纪出口中东的最常见瓷器。青瓷标志性的青釉可呈现不同的色调，包括这只碟子的灰绿色。其产地或为尼沙布尔，或为大不里士。

盘身为熔料制成。熔料又称石浆或石英浆，是中东制陶工人为应对仿制中国瓷器的难题而发展成的工艺，主要成分为磨砂或卵石制成的细石英粉，并在其中加入少量白黏土和一种作为熔料的玻璃物质。黏土赋予其可塑性，熔料经烧制后有助于物体凝固。（英国维多利亚与艾伯特博物馆）

Iranian green glazed dish with everted rim and impressed four fish design

15-16th Century, Height 6.8cm mouth diameter 34.7cm, Given by Sir Frank Brangwyn RA, The Victoria and Albert Museum, Britain

附12 龙泉窑青釉印双鱼纹洗残件

明永乐

高 7.4 厘米　口径 27 厘米　足径 17.4 厘米

龙泉大窑枫洞岩窑址出土

浙江省文物考古研究所藏

洗卷沿，圆唇，弧腹，圈足，足端较平或圆润，外底刮釉一圈。胎色灰白，胎壁较厚，釉色青灰，釉层凝厚。外底心微凹。沿面刻划卷草纹，内壁刻划海涛纹，内底刻划双鱼波浪纹，外壁下腹刻划莲瓣纹。外底刻有“官”字。（徐军）

Fragment of Longquan celadon dish impressed with twin fish design

Ming dynasty, Height 7.4cm mouth diameter 27cm foot diameter 17.4cm, Excavated from Fengdongyan kilnsite at Dayao village in Longquan, The Institute of Cultural Relics and Archaeology of Zhejiang Province

129 伊朗青釉刻划花草纹菱花口折沿盘

16 世纪

口径 38.7 厘米

英国维多利亚与艾伯特博物馆藏

此盘造型、釉色、纹饰均模仿当时盛行于中东市场的浙江龙泉窑青釉盘。龙泉青瓷在 14 ～ 15 世纪曾作为奢侈品被大量进口。此盘可能是在龙泉青瓷停止出口后伊朗仿制的替代品。（英国维多利亚与艾伯特博物馆）

Iranian celadon dish with bracket-lobed rim and carved and incised design of floral and grass

16th Century, Mouth diameter 38.7cm, The Victoria and Albert Museum, Britain

附13　龙泉窑青釉刻划折枝枇杷纹菱花式折沿盘

明早期

高 7.7 厘米　口径 47 厘米　足径 28.2 厘米

故宫博物院藏

盘通体呈菱花形。敞口，折沿，浅弧腹，圈足。盘内、外和圈足内均施青釉。外底有一圈涩胎无釉，系垫圈垫烧处。内底刻划折枝枇杷纹。

此盘造型和纹饰与明代永乐时期景德镇御窑烧造的青花盘相似，因此应属于明永乐时期龙泉窑烧造的宫廷用瓷。（黄卫文）

Longquan celadon dish with everted bracket-lobed rim and carved and incised loquat spray design

Early Ming dynasty, Height 7.7cm mouth diameter 47cm foot diameter 28.2cm, The Palace Museum

130 伊朗天蓝釉菊瓣纹折沿盘

17 世纪

高 6.6 厘米　口径 31.5 厘米

英国维多利亚与艾伯特博物馆藏

此盘是 17 世纪伊朗彩色陶瓷作品的典范。伊朗陶器通常使用单色釉，许多都带有压模或雕刻装饰，这只盘子的盘口也有类似装饰。

16 世纪伊朗制陶业规模并不大。直至 1600 年左右迁都伊斯法罕，对奢华餐具和墙砖的需求，开始促使各种风格与工艺的陶器迅速发展。

陶瓷器皿的制造中心现已不可考，现存作品展现出丰富的制陶工艺，如釉下彩、彩釉和 1650 年之后复兴的光泽釉。（英国维多利亚与艾伯特博物馆）

Iranian blue glazed dish with everted rim and chrysanthemum petals design

17th Century, Height 6.6cm mouth diameter 31.5cm, The Victoria and Albert Museum, Britain

附14 龙泉窑青釉刻菊瓣纹折沿洗

南宋至元

高 3.9 厘米　口径 13.4 厘米　足径 6.1 厘米

故宫博物院藏

洗敞口，折沿，浅弧腹，瘦底，圈足。内、外壁均刻菊瓣纹。洗内、外施青釉，圈足内亦施青釉。外底有一圈无釉，呈火石红色。（赵小春）

Longquan washer with everted rim and carved chrysanthemum petals design

From Southern Song dynasty to Yuan dynasty, Height 3.9cm mouth diameter 13.4cm foot diameter 6.1cm, The Palace Museum

附15 龙泉窑青釉刻菊瓣纹折沿盘

明早期

高 11 厘米 口径 45 厘米 足径 16 厘米

清宫旧藏

故宫博物院藏

盘敞口，折沿，浅弧壁，圈足。内、外和圈足内均施青釉，釉面莹润光亮。外底有一圈涩胎无釉，呈火石红色，系垫圈垫烧处。内壁刻菊瓣纹，外壁光素。

此盘形体较大，从造型和纹饰看，应属于明代永乐、宣德时期龙泉窑烧造的宫廷用瓷。（张涵）

Longquan dish with everted rim and carved chrysanthemum petals design

Early Ming dynasty, Height 11cm mouth diameter 45cm foot diameter 16cm, Collected by the Qing Palace, The Palace Museum

131 伊朗青釉镇

17 ~ 18 世纪

高 10.2 厘米　底径 10.8 厘米

英国维多利亚与艾伯特博物馆藏

在露台铺设优雅而轻盈的棉质、丝质帐子是莫卧儿宫廷典型的户外装饰。为防止地板上铺设的织物被风吹走，需在四角放置重物。这些重物被称作镇，亦名“地奴”，由石头、金属和玻璃等各种材质制成，通常四个一套，盛行于 17 世纪早期。陶瓷质的镇较为稀少，这套伊朗制品或为本土用品，或是供莫卧儿宫廷使用的出口品，具有沙阿 · 阿巴斯大帝统治下莫卧儿宫廷风格的本土化特征。（英国维多利亚与艾伯特博物馆）

Iranian celadon floor weight

17-18th Century, Height 10.2cm bottom diameter 10.8cm, The Victoria and Albert Museum, Britain

英国的仿龙泉青瓷

龙泉青瓷约在14世纪进入欧洲，但传入英国的数量有限。在英国收藏的中国瓷器中，年代最早且流传有序者正是龙泉青瓷。1532年，时任英国坎特伯雷大主教威廉姆·渥伦（William Warham）捐赠给牛津大学新学院（New College, Oxford University）一件龙泉青瓷碗，史称“渥伦碗”（Warham Bowl），现藏于牛津大学阿什莫林博物馆。

有记载显示，英国皇室收藏龙泉青瓷的时间应在19世纪。也是从那时起，收藏中国陶瓷逐渐成为英国贵族生活的时尚。工业革命带来的技术变革对英国陶瓷业产生深远影响，不但陶瓷产量因工业流水线技术而增加，窑炉建造和配釉技术也都有相应的突破。英国陶瓷工业对仿制中国陶瓷有浓厚兴趣并取得丰硕成果，20世纪英国皇家道尔顿（Royal Doulton）的产品是英国仿龙泉青瓷产品中的代表。

Imitations of Longquan Celadon Fired in Britain

The Longquan celadon entered Europe around the 14th century, but they were introduced to Britain in only limited number. Among the British collection of Chinese ceramics, the earliest and well-provenance piece is exactly Longquan celadon. In 1532, William Warham, the Archbishop of Canterbury, donated a Longquan celadon bowl to the New College, Oxford University. Known as the Warham Bowl, this piece is now in the collection of the Ashmolean Museum of Art and Archaeology, Oxford University.

History records demonstrate that the royal family of Britain started to collect Longquan celadon in the 19th century. It was also during this period that collecting Chinese ceramics gradually became fashionable among the British nobility. Changes in technology caused by the Industrial Revolution had profound impact on the ceramic industry in Britain. There was not only increase in the production output of ceramics due to the industrial streamlined manufacture, but also breakthroughs in kiln building and glaze recipe. The British ceramic industry had strong interest to copy Chinese ceramics and great accomplishments in this. The products of Royal Doulton fired in the 20th century is representative of Longquan style celadon made in Britain.

132 英国青釉杯

20 世纪

高 2.3 厘米　口径 7.5 厘米

英国大英博物馆藏

杯撇口，深腹，圈足。内、外和圈足内均施淡青色釉，釉面有浅开片。

原为海伦娜·莫特（1900 ~ 1997 年）旧藏，1997 年 10 月 22 日由伦敦邦瀚斯售出。该藏品为海伦娜·莫特从父亲处继承，其父是道尔顿艺术总监约瑟夫·莫特。（英国大英博物馆）

British celadon cup

20th Century, Height 2.3cm mouth diameter 7.5cm, The British Museum, Britain

专论

Essays

13 ~ 15 世纪伊斯兰地区对龙泉青瓷的仿制

[英] 奈杰尔·武德　英国威斯敏斯特大学（陶瓷专业荣誉教授）、牛津大学（考古学院荣誉研究员）
[英] 克里斯·多赫蒂　英国牛津大学

13 ~ 15 世纪，中国龙泉青瓷经由多条海上交通路线大量输出：一些向东到达了日本和韩国，另一些则向南运至越南和菲律宾，更多的龙泉青瓷继续向西到达了东南亚地区，诸如泰国、缅甸和斯里兰卡等国。此时期最长的贸易路线超过了 7000 海里（约 13000 公里），直至中东地区，满足了伊朗、叙利亚、埃及和伊拉克等诸多伊斯兰国家对龙泉青瓷的需求。霍尔木兹港（Hormuz）正是这些伊斯兰地区接收龙泉青瓷的主要港口。

如此广泛的国际贸易得以形成，有赖于位于浙江省西南、福建省北部岩石高地上体积庞大的龙窑，其以木柴为燃料，烧造了数以百万、质地坚硬且施厚釉的龙泉青瓷。这些龙泉青瓷烧造完成后，经河流运输至中国东海的海港，如宁波（宋时称明州、元时称庆元）、温州和泉州[1]。

来自中国的瓷器给接收这些瓷器的国家带来了深远的影响，促使当地（如日本、埃及）出现许多仿制龙泉青瓷的现象。中国龙泉青瓷在本土以外地区的仿制成为世界陶瓷史上一个重要的议题。

一　从东亚、东南亚地区的仿制谈起

东亚、东南亚地区国家拥有充足的、耐高温的土壤，因此当地窑工能够使用当地的瓷土和釉仿制龙泉青瓷（**图 1 ~ 图 4**）。有时，一些来自中国且了解青瓷制作工艺的工匠也会定居在这些国家，进一步帮助这些国家仿制龙泉青瓷[2]。尽管东南亚地区的仿龙泉瓷器也经过高温烧造，但受限于其所使用的瓷土的质量，其胎仍显得较为粗糙且玻化程度较低。同时，这些仿制品的釉也与龙泉窑瓷器釉的玉质光泽不同，或较薄且闪亮，或呈糖霜状而哑光。尽管如此，还是可以从这些仿制品中看到十分显著的龙泉窑瓷器风格特征。这一时期常见的仿制品器形主要是两类：一种类宽沿浅腹大盘，常装饰有辐射状分布的槽纹；另一类为较小的外壁饰有多面雕刻纹饰的莲瓣碗。

这一时期，向东出口至琉球、日本和朝鲜半岛的龙泉窑瓷器数量十分庞大，但这些地区对龙泉窑瓷器的仿制似乎并不是那么直接。自 13 世纪起，日本就是龙泉青瓷的重要市场之一，发现了 90 余处出土龙泉青瓷的地点[3]。然而，陶瓷技术在日本其实发展得很缓慢，尾张国（Owari Province，大约位于今爱知县的西部，是日本古代令制国之一，相当于中国古代的州或省）的濑户窑（Seto kilns）曾生产过一些简单的龙泉青瓷仿制品。直至 17 世纪，在琉球发现了适合制瓷的材料后，仿制龙泉青瓷才真正变得可行。其利用多室阶级龙窑（与龙窑一样也是依山而建，但是由多个窑室串联而成，烧造时更容易控制温度且使温度均匀），并用与中国龙泉瓷器相似的原材料和制作方式，生产出了一批中国境外最为成功的仿龙泉青瓷[4]。

朝鲜半岛地区虽然早已有了由越窑瓷器发展而来的复杂的青瓷传统，却对龙泉青瓷仿制较少。其中可能的原因

图 1　12 世纪　泰国西萨查那莱窑青釉刻划牡丹纹菱花口折沿盘
高 7.5 厘米　口径 29.5 厘米
英国维多利亚与艾伯特博物馆藏

图 2　1620 ~ 1640 年　日本有田窑青釉壶
高 18.5 厘米　口径 15 厘米
英国牛津大学阿什莫林博物馆藏

图 3　918 ~ 1392 年　高丽青釉菱花口折沿盘
高 2.5 厘米　口径 10.2 厘米
英国维多利亚与艾伯特博物馆藏

图 4　13 世纪　龙泉窑青釉模印贴花双鱼纹折沿盘残件
高 5 厘米　口径 22 厘米
英国牛津大学阿什莫林博物馆藏

是，其食物及饮食传统决定了他们并不太需要龙泉窑器形的餐具（如龙泉窑中常见的大盘）。如果仅从外形来看，有一类高丽青釉莲瓣碗会被人们误认为是对龙泉青瓷的仿制。然而，这些高丽青釉莲瓣碗主要生产于 12 世纪早期，比龙泉青瓷相似产品早近 1 个世纪，说明其不可能是龙泉青瓷的仿制品。事实上，这些莲瓣碗可能是仿定窑白瓷，后者早在 10 世纪末期便开始出现莲瓣碗类器形[5]。

图 5　宋　龙泉窑青釉模印贴花双鱼纹折沿洗
故宫博物院藏

图 6　宋　龙泉窑青釉模印贴花双鱼纹折沿洗
故宫博物院藏

二　中东地区仿制中国陶瓷

在“全球范围对龙泉青瓷的仿制”这一议题下，还有一个重要但较鲜为人知的研究主题，便是中东地区对龙泉青瓷的仿制。中东的龙泉青瓷仿制品可能是 13 ~ 17 世纪埃及、波斯和叙利亚的一些窑厂生产的。尽管这些中东地区的仿龙泉青瓷器仍有诸多尚未明确的问题，但其生产数量甚大，占据了同时期中东地区生产的所有釉陶产品相当大的比例，这是有目共睹的。

中东地区陶工在瓷器生产中面临的最大问题就是缺乏耐高温的原材料——当地主要产出的是一种低熔点的钙质陶土。而中东地区如何使用本土原料经低温烧造以仿制高温烧造的瓷器正是本研究主题中的重要论题，因为许多中东龙泉青瓷仿制品的釉质、釉色和器形在外观上都达到了与龙泉青瓷极其相似的程度。然而，另有一些仿制品的釉色更接近蓝绿色（即更接近早期中东地区陶瓷器的传统釉色），而不是龙泉窑常见的青绿釉色，还有一些仿制品的器形实际是中东地区传统的金属器的器形（**图 5 ~ 图 10**）。所有这些不寻常的“中东青瓷”引发了诸多关于其制作、施釉和烧制的疑问。本文就将重点探索这些技术应对层面的问题。

图 7　1450 ~ 1550 年
伊朗青釉印四鱼纹折沿盘（尼沙普尔或泰伯里，熔块胎）
高 6.8 厘米　口径 34.7 厘米
英国维多利亚与艾伯特博物馆藏

图 8　16 世纪　伊朗青釉刻划花草纹菱花口折沿盘（熔块胎）
口径 38.7 厘米
英国维多利亚与艾伯特博物馆藏

（　）中东地区仿制中国陶瓷的先锋——伊拉克

中东地区仿制中国陶瓷的技术是古已有之的。9 世纪，伊拉克地区在陶瓷的仿制和创新上取得了重大突破（尽管目前尚未发现相关窑址）。其仿制的中国陶瓷器包括唐代

图 9　伊利汗国（1256 ~ 1353 年）
伊朗青釉印三鱼纹折沿盘（熔块胎）
高 6.8 厘米　口径 35 厘米
英国牛津大学阿什莫林博物馆藏

图 10　12 ~ 13 世纪
伊朗青釉印鱼纹高足敛口碗（熔块胎）
高 7.6 厘米　口径 14.3 厘米
英国维多利亚与艾伯特博物馆藏

图 11　15 世纪（马穆鲁克王朝）
埃及青釉刻花草纹菱花口折沿盘（厚釉浅黄陶土胎）
高 7.7 厘米　口径 36.5 厘米
大英博物馆藏

北方白釉陶瓷器（包括那些经高温烧造的白瓷）和多彩陶瓷器（包括来自北方的三彩陶器和南方的长沙窑陶瓷器）[6]。这些伊拉克陶仿制品展示了当地陶工如何运用精湛的技艺使本土材料呈现出中国陶瓷的特征，这是一项难度倍增的任务，因为当地陶工使用的是与中国陶瓷完全不同的原材料。而在此之前，中东地区鲜有精美的釉陶，在这些伊拉克釉陶上体现出的试验和创新，为后世中东陶瓷器（尤其是锡釉陶器）风格的形成奠定了技术基础。

（二）福斯塔特留下的珍宝

本文主要研究对象为福斯塔特（Fustat）遗址（位于埃及开罗附近）出土的陶器残片。这些陶器残片现存牛津大学考古与艺术史研究实验室（The Research Laboratory for Archaeology and the History of Art at Oxford University），是美国科学家和考古学家亚历山大 · 卡其马奇克（Alexander Kaczmarczyk）在 20 世纪 70 年代末至 80 年代初采集的，其年代大致为马穆鲁克苏丹国时期（Mamluk Sultanate，1250 ~ 1517 年，是阿拉伯人于埃及建立的王朝，国家宗教为伊斯兰教）[7]。

马穆鲁克苏丹国的首都开罗位于福斯塔特北面，在法蒂玛王朝(Fatimid，969 年 ~ 1171 年)和阿尤布王朝(Ayyubid，1171 ~ 1250 年）时期为一个占地很大、有护城墙的城市。13 世纪中期，福斯塔特成为此区域的工业中心和繁荣的港口（主要处理自红海进口的奢侈品贸易）。至 1340 年左右，福斯塔特的人口数量已达 50 万，这个繁荣、有活力的伊斯兰世界贸易和文化中心进口了当时已知世界的各个角落的纺织品、金属器、陶瓷和玻璃器。然而，福斯塔特在 14 世纪中期便迅速衰落（可能与 1347 年流行的瘟疫有关），因此前述牛津大学所藏的大多数陶器残片的时代应为 13 世纪中期到 14 世纪中期之间，而这一时期也恰是中国龙泉青瓷生产的鼎盛时期。卡其马奇克收集的这批陶瓷碎片中约有 20 件仿东亚青瓷，此次研究选用了其中的 9 件。

日本考古研究队自 20 世纪 60 年代便开始在福斯塔特遗址做发掘工作，并对福斯塔特出土文物的背景进行了详细研究。其中发现了许多中国陶瓷碎片，包括龙泉青瓷、耀州窑类型的瓷器、青白瓷和卵白釉瓷，所有这些中国陶瓷都成为中东陶工模仿的对象[8]。而在福斯塔特发现的中国瓷器仿制品似乎以仿制龙泉青瓷为主，弓场纪知（Tadanori）记录到："在福斯塔特仓库中共有 1677 箱马穆鲁克时期陶瓷器，几乎所有箱里都包含有绿色釉陶，显示了龙泉青瓷对同时期埃及陶瓷器的重要影响。"（图 11）[9]

此外，发现于福斯塔特的 13 ~ 16 世纪时期的中国陶瓷也以青瓷为主（其余都为景德镇青花瓷），龙泉窑瓷器的比例占到了总量的 87% 左右[10]。这一比重也适用于在东非肯尼亚发现的龙泉瓷器："近期被中国考古学家研究的来自肯尼亚三十八个遗址的九千五百五十二片陶瓷碎片，年代在公元十四到十五世纪期间，龙泉窑瓷器占据了百分之八十三到八十九的中国陶瓷器总量。"[11] 大量的中国青瓷在波斯湾入口处的霍尔木兹岛被发现。霍尔木兹是 14 世纪起中东地区进口中国陶瓷的主要港口之一。它就像一座青瓷的坟场，德里克 · 肯尼特（Derek Kennet）指出，数量惊人的龙泉青瓷在此被发现，"甚至在最低级别的乡村地区"[12]。近年来在霍尔木兹发现的一些高质量的龙泉青瓷碎片"与在龙泉枫洞岩窑址（临近龙泉大窑遗址）发现的贡御青瓷相似"，据推测，"在霍尔木兹岛发现的明代早期中国陶瓷碎片可能是郑和远航中进行的非正规贸易和交换的结果"[13]。

（三）扑朔迷离：中东龙泉青瓷仿制品的模本

前文已谈及，中东地区发现的大量中国青瓷只是广泛的海上陶瓷贸易的一个方面，浙江省有多达上百个服务于外销青瓷的窑场[14]。同时，也有很多江苏、福建和广东的瓷窑址生产越窑和龙泉窑类型的产品，促进了海上贸易[15]。龙泉窑瓷器拥有异常坚硬的胎体，且施以质地坚硬、由二价铁离子和三价铁离子着色的淡绿色高温厚釉。如此高的质量使他们成为理想的贸易商品。从东南亚海域发现的两艘沉船——10 世纪的井里汶沉船（Cirabon shipwreck）和约 1400 年的"龙泉"沉船（"Longquan" wreck），就可一窥当时中国青瓷出口贸易的规模[16]。井里汶沉船发现于爪哇海西岸，

图 12　13 ~ 15 世纪　缅甸伊洛瓦底三角洲窑青釉篦划花纹盘
高 7 厘米　口径 25.4 厘米
美国弗利尔美术馆藏

图 13　13 世纪　龙泉窑青釉器残件
斯里兰卡沉船遗址打捞
美国牛津大学阿什莫林博物馆藏

图 14　埃及福斯塔特仿制青瓷废品标本
牛津大学考古与艺术史研究实验室藏

载有约 10 万件越窑瓷器和约 4 万件中国白瓷[17]。“龙泉”沉船发现于马来西亚东海岸，其巨大的残存船体（长 30 余米）上载有约 10 万件陶瓷器：40% 为中国青瓷，40% 为泰国青瓷，剩余 20% 为泰国彩绘陶瓷。

正如“龙泉”沉船的货物组成显示的那样，许多东南亚仿龙泉青瓷产品也常和中国青瓷一起向西大量输出。例如由日本金泽大学（Kanazawa University）的佐佐木达夫（Tatsuo Sasaki）和佐佐木森英（Hanae Sasaki）主持发掘的阿拉伯联合酋长国祖尔法 (Jolfar) 遗址就出土了东南亚的仿龙泉青瓷产品[18]。对祖尔法遗址出土的部分仿龙泉青瓷与来自泰国北部与缅甸南部的窑址中出土的青瓷进行比较，其岩相分析（用于分析材料制品的物相组成和显微结构特征的研究，可了解陶瓷胎中的矿物种类、粒径大小、分布情况以及瓷釉的玻璃化程度和微观结构等信息）显示，这些祖尔法遗址出土的仿龙泉青瓷是来自 13 世纪末到 15 世纪初缅甸南部窑址（端迪镇 Twante Village）的(图 12、图 13)[19]。因此，一个令人困惑的问题出现了：一些时代稍晚的中东青瓷究竟是对龙泉青瓷本身的仿制，还是对龙泉窑仿制品的仿制？比如泰国与缅甸的仿龙泉窑制品，甚至是其他中东地区的龙泉窑仿制品，毕竟龙泉青瓷的风格在中东地区流行甚广。

关于中东地区的陶瓷烧造窑址问题，前述卡其马奇克收集的 20 件仿青瓷碎片中，有 6 片是烧至变形或有瑕疵的废品，因此可以推断这 6 片是埃及当地制造的(图 14)。6 片中有 3 片为白色的熔块胎陶（Stonepaste，或称 fritware，中东地区常见的一类胎体，后文会给出详细的解释），还有 3 片为浅棕色硅质胎体。至于其他 14 片，因为福斯塔特是当时的贸易中心，所以其有可能是埃及制造，也有可能来自波斯（即今伊朗）或叙利亚。因此关于本文将要研究的样品（出土于福斯塔特遗址的灰坑），其来源尚不能确定。事实上，现今我们对伊斯兰世界生产的仿制青瓷（即使其是此时伊斯兰世界最为流行的陶瓷风格之一）状况所知甚少，即使这是此时期伊斯兰世界最为流行的陶瓷风格之一。中东地区仿青瓷制品不仅流行在马穆鲁克苏丹国的领土上（即埃及和叙利亚），也流行在与之相邻的蒙古汗国中（主要指波斯地区）[20]。

三　胎釉分析与结果——从配料到烧造

本次分析是在前述国际贸易、当地仿制和考古发现的背景下进行的，选取了卡其马奇克在福斯塔特遗址收集的 9 片陶瓷片，主要运用了扫描电子显微镜（Combined scanning electron microscopy，简称 SEM，被运用在显示胎体和釉的结构上）和能量色散 X 射线谱分析（Energy dispersive analysis，简称 EDA，用于分析陶瓷胎釉的化学元素）技术，研究其胎体和釉质的成分范围(图 15，表 1、表 2)。

图 15　本次研究分析的福斯塔特出土的马穆鲁克时期仿制中国青瓷标本及编号
牛津大学考古与艺术史研究实验室藏

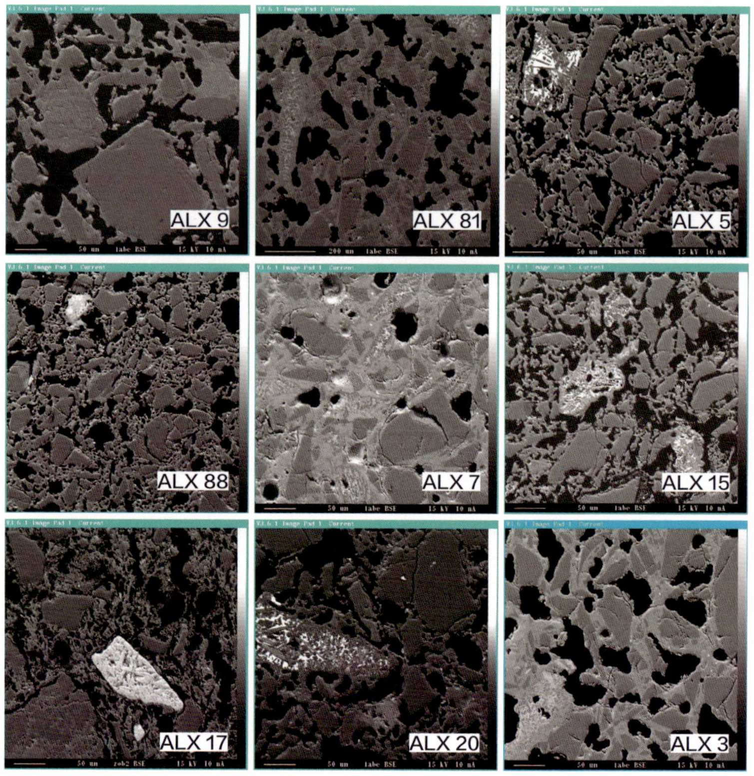

图 16　质量不同的熔块胎陶胎体的背散射扫描电子显微镜（SEM）图像
（图中显示了胎体的结构和物相，深灰色区域为石英，浅灰色区域为间质性玻璃，大块颗粒为半熔化的含有些许氧化铅的玻璃体）

表 1　福斯塔特遗址出土的马穆鲁克时期青釉陶瓷碎片胎体成分表

	ALX9	ALX81	ALX5	ALX88	ALX7	ALX15	ALX17	ALX20	ALX3
SiO_2	87.9	89.8	82.4	84.9	80.5	88.6	75.7	85.8	88.0
Al_2O_3	1.5	2.7	10.4	6.8	6.4	4.0	6.8	6.2	3.8
Fe_2O_3	1.1	0.7	1.1	1.1	1.6	0.8	3.0	1.2	0.9
TiO_2	0.2	0.3	0.6	0.6	0.6	0.4	0.5	0.6	0.3
CaO	5.8	3.9	1.2	1.0	5.7	2.9	9.7	2.3	3.4
MgO	1.6	0.4	0.4	0.3	0.7	1.0	1.6	0.6	0.4
K_2O	1.0	0.5	1.3	1.2	0.8	0.9	1.3	0.8	0.7
Na_2O	1.2	1.8	2.2	3.5	3.0	1.0	1.1	1.9	2.2
MnO	0	0.1	0.1	0	0.1	0.1	0.1	0.1	0.1
PbO	0	0	0.4	0.8	0.8	0.3	0.2	0.4	0.2
总计	100.3	100.2	100.1	100.2	100.2	100	100	99.9	100

表 2　福斯塔特遗址出土的马穆鲁克时期青釉陶瓷碎片釉层成分表

	ALX 9	ALX 81	ALX 5	ALX 88	ALX 7	ALX 15	ALX 17	ALX 20	ALX 3
SiO_2	65.0	60.2	61.8	58.9	52.2	50.3	50.1	49.9	47.0
Al_2O_3	3.0	7.4	1.6	3.6	2.7	3.7	2.8	2.7	1.0
Fe_2O_3	1.9	5.0	0.9	1.9	1.5	2.5	1.8	4.5	1.8
TiO_2	0.4	1.2	0.2	0.4	0.3	0.4	0.4	0.4	0.1
CaO	8.0	5.1	10.4	4.6	2.5	2.9	4.4	3.0	4.2
MgO	3.1	2.2	3.0	1.8	1.1	1.9	1.2	1.6	2.4
K_2O	3.1	3.3	1.8	2.0	1.1	1.6	2.9	0.8	0.6
Na_2O	11.7	9.6	8.5	6.6	5.7	8.0	5.8	6.4	6.6
MnO	0.1	0.1	0.1	0.1	0	0.1	0.1	0.1	0
P_2O_5	0.7	0.5	0.3	0.3	0.3	0.3	0.4	0.6	0.2
PbO	0.1	2.8	6.9	15.6	23.2	24.0	25.0	25.9	28.4
SnO_2	0	0	2.0	0.5	6.0	2.3	0.1	2.5	6.4
CuO	0.8	0.5	0	1.1	0.2	0.3	3.8	0.1	0.3
CoO	0	0.022	0.09	0.022	0.012	0.018	0.009	0.023	0.016
NiO	0	0	0	0.1	0	0	0	0.1	0
ZnO	0	0	0.1	0	0	0.2	0	0	0.1
Sb_2O_5	0	0	0.1	0	0.1	0.1	0	0	0
AsO_2	0	0	0	0.1	0	0	0	0.1	0
SO_3	0.2	0.1	0.1	0	0	0	0	0	0
BaO	0.01	0.02	0.03	0.03	0.04	0.04	0.07	0.04	0.01
总计	98.17	97.9	97.7	97.53	96.84	98.46	98.87	98.76	99.16

（一）胎体的化学成分和结构

中东的仿青瓷产品与中国所产的龙泉青瓷有一个主要的区别：中东地区的仿制品实际是使用人工合成的、富含石英并以玻璃作为助熔剂的陶器，这种胎体被称为熔块胎陶。熔块胎陶作为胎体材料在11世纪早期的波斯就已出现，随后逐渐被整个伊斯兰世界用于制作精致的陶器，至今仍被广泛使用[21]。

成书于1301年，由阿布·卡西姆·卡萨尼（Abu' lQasimKashani，蒙古宫廷历史学家，也是喀山著名陶艺家族的一员）撰写的波斯陶器制造著作中记录了熔块胎陶的配方：10份粉碎的石英，1份玻璃粉末和1份黏土[22]。而采用熔块胎陶制作器皿的时间，恰好与中东地区大量出现中国陶瓷（如白瓷和龙泉窑瓷器）的时间吻合。福斯塔特出土陶瓷碎片的分析显示，其胎体为高硅质胎体（硅的质量百分数含量为75.7% ~ 89.8%），且常见未熔化或半熔化的玻璃颗粒、间质性玻璃（interstitial glass）和少量钙质黏土残留，这些都证明福斯塔特出土陶瓷的胎体制作使用了熔块胎陶（图16）[23]。

熔块胎陶具有明显的硅质胎体特征，并常伴有玻璃质和颗粒质的断口[24]，这或许表明石英（二氧化硅）和玻璃是当地用以仿制中国瓷器的原材料。然而，熔块胎陶在结构上远比它所模仿的龙泉瓷器要脆弱，因为其缺少针状莫来石晶体（mullite）——一种普遍存在于大多数中国高温瓷器的物质，可以增加其自身强度[25]。

在福斯塔特出土陶瓷碎片的胎体成分表中（见表1），氧化钠的含量（质量百分数为1.1% ~ 3.5%）指示了玻璃成分（玻璃的主要成分为氧化硅、氧化钠及其他氧化物）。此外，9件陶瓷样品中有7件含有氧化铅（质量百分数为0.2% ~ 0.8%左右），通过此含量并结合斑点分析（测试矿物成分的一种方法）表明氧化铅是来自样品胎体内半熔化的玻璃颗粒。胎体成分中的氧化钙则应与石灰碱玻璃和钙质黏土有关。然而，每一陶瓷碎片的化学成分（氧化硅类型、添加的玻璃成分及数量）、原料的粉碎程度、原料的纯净度都不同，说明中东陶工在利用主体为熔块胎陶的配方之下还有着许多操作上的细微差别（见图15）。而这也许不是简单的地质差异上的问题，因为在福斯塔特出土的陶瓷废品（可能是福斯塔特当地烧造的，应都使用的是本地原料）也显示出了不同的胎体成分（见图14）。

（二）釉的原料与配方

本次研究也对马穆鲁克时期青釉陶瓷碎片的釉层成分进行了分析研究。中东地区釉的制作发展与其玻璃制作传统紧密相连，前者就是从后者发展而来的[26]。在原材料方面，即使地中海和中东地区的玻璃器在成分上通常十分相似，但也显示出了差异显著的制作方式。其中一种制作方式，是将富含二氧化硅的材料与高钠蒸发盐矿物材料（例如古代湖泊里的盐）混合，这种方法的使用典型是古罗马玻璃器。第二种制作方式是将二氧化硅与富含钠的草木灰混合，这是伊斯兰玻璃以及之后的威尼斯玻璃的典型配方。钙元素是石灰碱玻璃或石灰碱釉中的第三种必要元素（其他两种元素为硅和钠），古罗马玻璃中的钙元素通常来自含有贝壳的沙子，伊斯兰玻璃中的钙元素则来自草木灰。因此，许多传统中东和地中海地区的玻璃主要采用的是二元配方（例如将钙质沙子与高钠蒸发盐混合，或将硅质岩石与高钠草木灰混合），虽然最终熔化后的成分相当于三部分（二氧化硅、氧化钠和氧化钙）的混合，即通常所知的钠钙玻璃[27]。

前述波斯喀山学者阿布·卡西姆·卡萨尼记录了利用第二种玻璃器的制作方式：将粉碎的二氧化硅和高钠草木灰构成的混合物碾成细末来做釉。这种方法基本上可视为利用玻璃的制作工艺来制作釉[28]。中东工匠制釉还存在另一种常见的情况，即将一种粉状的玻璃体"锡灰"（氧化铅和氧化锡的混合物）加入钠钙玻璃的制作配方中，随后一起被熔化，再研磨成粉末状，用以制造出精致不透明的白色釉。在波斯，这种不透明白色釉通常在拉斯特彩（lustre-painting，伊斯兰釉上彩的一个重要品种，其特点是图案在器物表面散发出明显的金属光泽）中使用[29]。

（三）釉的主要成分

将本次考察研究的9片马穆鲁克青釉陶瓷片釉层的主要成分，按氧化铅含量由低到高排列成图表可知（图17）[30]，

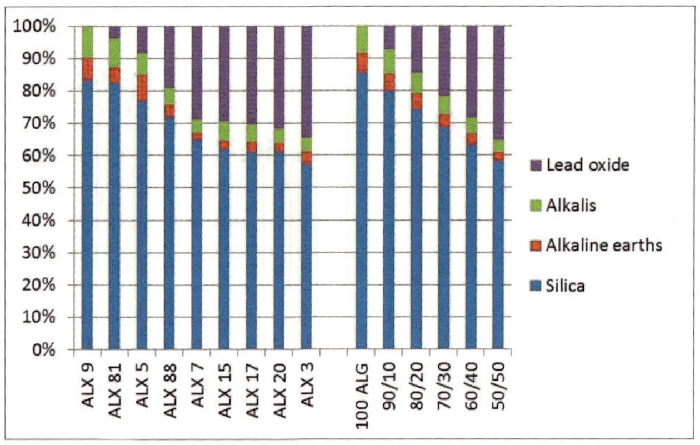

图17 马穆鲁克青釉陶瓷的釉层主要成分图表

图 18 典型马穆鲁克青瓷釉成分

从上至下成分组成为：94 份钠钙灰玻璃 +6 份氧化锡；71 份钠钙玻璃 +23 份二硅酸铅 +6 份氧化锡 ;47 份钠钙玻璃 +47 份二硅酸铅 +6 份氧化锡。实验的燃烧条件为氧化气氛中烧至六号奥吞锥温度。

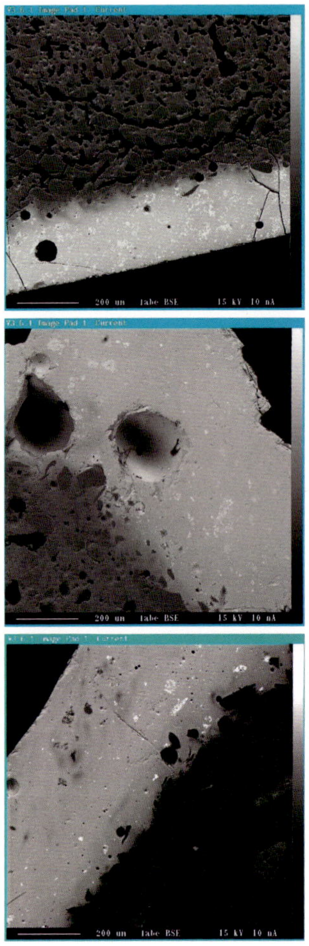

图 19 马穆鲁克青瓷釉背散射 SEM 图像

样品编号从上至下为：ALX 5，ALX 7 和 ALX 15，图像显示了氧化锡颗粒，即白色斑点

样品 ALX9 的釉层中不含有铅，基本属于钠钙玻璃，而有 6 片含有质量 20% ~ 28% 的氧化铅。另一点值得注意的是，当氧化铅含量上升时，二氧化硅的含量便下降。事实上，这次所测得的釉层成分的区间范围包含了从钠钙玻璃至硅、铅、铅氧化物的共晶混合物（Eutectic，是指由两种或多种元素组成的、能在比各组分熔点更低的温度下形成单一化合物，由此制造的釉通常具有很好的化学稳定性、较低的熔点等优点）。前者是高硅含量的复合物，而后者的二氧化硅含量较低，因此二氧化硅含量在釉层成分中呈现出逐渐下降的趋势。釉层主要成分图表中还可看出本文分析的马穆鲁克青釉陶瓷片釉层的成分与钠钙玻璃、铅玻璃组成的混合物（即图表中的右组所示）的关系——这些釉中的铅含量止于 50% 的钠钙玻璃和 50% 的铅玻璃（主要为二硅酸铅，lead bisilicate）混合后的所显示成分，而多数釉的成分在钠钙玻璃和铅玻璃配比为 6:4 到 5:5 的区间内[31]。在实际生产中，工匠可能采用了经机械搅磨成粉的钠钙玻璃与粉末状的富锡、铅的铅碱玻璃依据不同比例混合制成釉，这正与阿布 · 卡西姆的记录相似。

（四）烧造温度

许多中东传统陶瓷对釉的制作都力求达到前述共晶混合物的状态，而这经常需要通过大量的实验才能达成。当釉的结构如前述背散射 SEM 图像的右组中显示那样有少量的氧化锡（质量百分数为 6%）且在氧化气氛中烧成而出现不透明状态时，其最终的烧成温度在六号奥吞锥（Orton Cone 06，995° C，每小时 60°C；或 1010° C，每小时 150°C）左右。这应就是本次考察的 9 片釉陶的烧造温度范围（图 18）。

（五）氧化锡的应用

从马穆鲁克时期青釉陶瓷碎片釉层成分表可知，本次研究的 9 片马穆鲁克青釉陶瓷中有 5 片含有氧化锡，质量百分数为 2% ~ 6%。前述已提及，氧化锡可以使伊斯兰陶瓷器的釉变白、变不透明。最初，这种釉被用来仿制中国瓷器或带有白色化妆土的炻器，以及长沙窑的一些陶瓷器类型[32]。用锡元素制造的不透明釉在中东地区也被用来作为陶瓷绘制的白色背景，从而绘制拉斯特彩或绿色（氧化铜为主要着色剂）、蓝色（氧化钴为主要着色剂）纹饰[33]。然而，笔者在研究 9 ~ 10 世纪伊拉克萨马拉（Samarra）遗址出土的陶瓷时[34]，发现了氧化锡更为具体的使用方式：一片伊拉克当地仿长沙窑高温琥珀色釉的釉陶釉层中含有 2% 的氧化锡，从而呈现出中国灰釉的朦胧之效。因此，氧化锡并不总是和白釉联系在一起。在中东陶瓷中，氧化锡也被大量使用在青瓷仿制品中，本文所研究的马穆鲁克青釉陶瓷中就利用了氧化锡以模仿龙泉青釉的玉质半透明效果（图 19）。

图 20 由氧化铁和氧化铜着色的马穆鲁克青瓷标本
可能在约 1000℃的氧化气氛中烧造

图 21 含氧化铁、二氧化钛的石灰碱釉在 1250℃的还原气氛烧造后的成色，氧化铁含量相同（1.5%）、二氧化钛含量不同的釉所呈现的颜色，从左至右釉中含有 0 ~ 0.8% 二氧化钛

（六）釉的厚度

中东陶工使用的另一模仿龙泉青瓷釉特征的技法是施厚釉，本文研究的 9 片釉陶平均釉层厚度在 0.6 毫米，甚至可与龙泉青瓷本身釉的厚度（通常在 0.4 ~ 1.7 毫米）相提并论[35]。龙泉瓷器的厚釉是通过多次施釉达到的[36]，中东釉陶则没有显示出多次施釉，因此这些马穆鲁克青瓷的釉的厚度是如何实现的现在仍然未知，其中一种可能性是在制釉悬浮液中加入了胶体。

图 22 ALX 3 显示出轻度还原效果 样品釉面气泡和发黑都为氧化铅导致

（七）釉的着色

中东地区陶工在模仿进口中国青瓷釉时面临着模仿高温釉的技术难题，中国的高温釉是大约在 1240℃的还原气氛中烧造而成的，由铁离子和钛离子着色[37]。二价铁离子的自然色加上少量三价铁离子，在高温釉中且含量低于 2% 的情况下，就可使釉呈现出冰蓝色[38]。然而，当釉中氧化钛含量高于 0.2% 时，釉色会变绿；随着氧化钛含量的升高，釉色愈加变绿[39]（图 20、图 21），这可能是由于在还原气氛中钛离子会对二价铁离子造成氧化作用，最终使釉中的三价铁离子（自身为琥珀色）的比例增加，使蓝釉变绿[40]。氧化钛是东亚、东南亚地区制釉原料中非常常见的天然杂质，因此显绿色的青瓷远远多于显蓝色的青瓷。

东亚、东南亚地区的窑炉温度可达 900℃ ~ 1200℃，且烧造时为还原气氛，这在伊斯兰陶瓷的烧造中是见不到的，即使伊斯兰陶工已认识到了这一烧造条件。这是因为这些伊斯兰陶瓷的釉中含有氧化铅，会导致其在还原气氛中起泡、变黑（此效果在编号 ALX3 的样品上最为明显，图 22）。伊斯兰拉斯特彩陶烧造中会采用还原气氛，但是作用在未烧造的釉上颜料上，并且烧造温度低于釉的熔点（基本在 500℃ ~ 600℃）[41]。

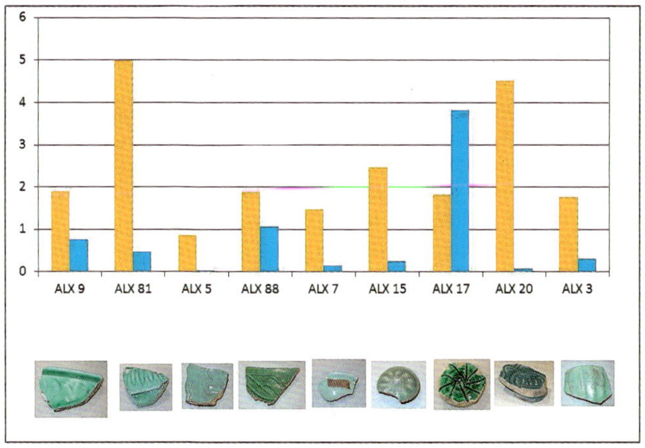

图 23 不同铁氧化物和铜氧化物含量与釉色关系图
显示了本次研究的 9 件样品中釉所含铁氧化物（黄色）和铜氧化物（蓝色）的重量百分比

依据马穆鲁克时期青釉陶瓷碎片釉层成分表的结果显示（见表 2），伊斯兰陶工在仿制中国青瓷颜色时采取的主要措施是：在氧化气氛中，将氧化铁和氧化铜在釉中熔融以提供三价铁离子和二价铜离子。三价铁离子呈琥珀色，二价铜离子呈蓝绿色（或在铅含量更高的釉里呈翠绿色）。也就是说，氧化铁和氧化铜按照不同比例被混合以使釉呈现不同程度的青色（图 23）。

（八）釉着色的另一实例：氧化钴的使用

本次研究的 9 片马穆鲁克青瓷样品中有 7 片氧化铜含量超过了 0.2%，这一含量足

图 24　摩洛哥马拉喀什近郊现代窑炉
其设计与容量与中世纪中东地区窑炉类似（奈杰尔·武德摄）

图 25　15 世纪早期　龙泉枫洞岩窑（大窑）产品
此盘明显有两种釉色，釉面大部分区域被氧化呈琥珀色，仅右上角小部分区域是在充分还原气氛下得以呈青翠色

以使釉具淡蓝绿色，同时使釉中的氧化铁变得更绿。然而，在编号 ALX5 和 ALX20 这两件样品中，氧化铜的含量过低（分别是 0 和 0.1%），无法在氧化焰中提供任何显著的颜色。然而这两片的釉色仍很绿（见图 15、图 23），这就要归功于氧化钴了（氧化钴在大多数样品中都被检测到，在这两片中的含量分别为 0.9% 和 0.2%）。尽管所测得的氧化钴含量在数值上是本次测试采用的技术手段中可探测得到的最低值，但相较于几乎为零的氧化铜含量，足可说明这两片样品的釉确是由氧化铁和低含量的氧化钴共同着色的，而不是常见的氧化铁和氧化铜的组合着色。

（九）伊斯兰陶瓷烧造的窑炉

另一个值得考虑的生产细节是伊斯兰陶瓷的烧造。有关中世纪伊斯兰陶瓷的生产窑址极少被发掘，但少数已被发现的伊斯兰陶瓷窑炉有着大致相同的风格：拱顶结构，内部高约 2 米，建在有孔的地面上，其下置一个巨大的火塘；轮辐状的悬桁架（杆与杆结成的铰链结构）支撑着窑室内烧造的器皿，火焰最后从拱顶的空隙中散走。这类窑炉在西班牙的安达卢西亚佩奇纳（pechina）、乌兹别克斯坦的塔什干等地多有发现（图 24）[42]。前述阿布·卡西姆的书中也记录了这种窑炉："这些支架置于窑中，在阿拉伯语中叫作 'shakhureh'，当地叫作 'dam' 或 'dasht'。它就像一个高塔一样，内部有成排的烧制过的陶钉固定在墙上的孔中。被烧制的器皿置于其上，经历 12 个小时热量充足稳定的烧造。烧造中规定：直至烟停才可加入木柴，因此烟并未破坏或使器皿变黑。"[43] 与同时期中国的龙泉龙窑一次可烧造上千件陶瓷相比，这些小型窑炉一次最多可能只烧造几百件陶瓷[44]。

（十）烧制过程中的能源消耗

另一点也应被注意的是，伊斯兰地区在生产精细釉陶过程中所需的巨大的能源消耗问题，包括人工和植物燃料的消耗。这一问题与中东地区的仿制青瓷传统密切相关。

在燃料消耗方面，首先出现的需求是从沙漠植物中获得灰烬以制造陶瓷胎体和釉所需的熔块。对早期配方的研究和对釉本身的研究显示，多达一半的釉的配方是富含钠的草木灰与粉碎的硅质岩石搅拌在一起，二者的混合体被熔化成液态。这个过程要在高温中持续 8 小时左右，要消耗大量燃料。同时，仿制青瓷通常需要准备锡灰，并在其熔化后进行数小时的氧化，然后再加入富含铅、锡的熔块中，这一过程需要更多的燃料。而富含锡的熔块本身就需要将锡灰加到钠钙玻璃中，并在窑炉内再次熔化，而此过程需要 12 小时[45]。

其次，青瓷仿制品的釉比普通锡釉更厚，因此其生产需要更多的釉材料。施釉后的烧制也需要更多的植物燃料。尽管中东地区的仿青瓷制品通常是在当地被使用，而不是像龙泉青瓷一样参与国际贸易，其生产过程也需要大量的当地燃料，但是中东地区本身植被是十分匮乏的。

此外，原料的需求也十分巨大。硅质岩石需要被粉碎成细灰，熔化的玻璃体需要在窑炉中被搅拌。之后这些玻璃体被倒入冷水中碎成小块，被捣烂和研磨。铅和锡被同时氧化，随后这些金属在熔化状态下被混合在一起。熔化了的富含锡的玻璃体被舀入水中弄碎为后续的研磨做准备。阿布·卡西姆的著作中也描述了这一过程，似乎这些混合、粉碎和研磨的过程是人工完成的，而不是依赖水碓（利用河流动力推进水轮转动，从而拨动碓杆粉碎制瓷原料），后者正是龙泉青瓷生产作坊所使用的生产工具[46]。

（十一）潜在的毒性：铅元素的释放

关于釉的最后一个问题就是釉的潜在毒性。釉中的氧化铜会以百倍的速度增加铅元素的释放[47]，文献中记载了多起由此导致的铅中毒的例子[48]。通过检测中国铜绿铅釉的铅元素释放，结果显示其中的铅含量存在潜在的危险[49]。因此，一些马穆鲁克时期的仿制青瓷也可能遇到同样的问题。然而，龙泉青瓷在中东地区拥有“遇到有毒食物会变色”的名声，这恰好与检测结果相悖。产生这一名声实际可能是因为龙泉青瓷盘通常在烧造还原不充分的时候呈琥珀色（图25）。事实上，烧制后的龙泉釉是出了名的高稳定和抗化学侵蚀，因此在烧造完成后想要有釉色的改变是不可能的。反而是中东地区仿青瓷器皿中会加入铅元素，带来潜在的中毒危险，但中东的人们却并不怀疑他们自身所产的器皿存在潜在的毒性。

结论

中东地区仿制中国龙泉青瓷是伊斯兰陶瓷史上很重要的研究主题。以长达几个世纪的使用当地材料仿制中国陶瓷的经验为基础，伊斯兰陶工在13～17世纪生产了仿龙泉青瓷制品，正如同一时期东南亚和东亚陶工进行的成功仿制一样。虽然中东陶工面临着特殊的挑战，如当地缺乏合适的陶土原料、烧造条件难以达到等，以及对中国本身制瓷技术的几乎一无所知。然而，通过采取熔块胎陶为胎体和对不透明锡釉的调试，中东陶工成功生产出了仿龙泉青瓷产品。通过熟练混合氧化铁和氧化铜（有时还有氧化钴）等着色剂，这类仿制品能够在一定程度上与龙泉青瓷的釉色极为相似；并且就如龙泉青瓷一样，当地的仿制品也被施以厚釉。在成分上，中东地区仿龙泉青瓷的釉处于钠钙玻璃到铅共晶混合物的区间范围内，烧造温度约为1000℃。

现在已知的是，中东生产的仿龙泉制品在13～15世纪都很流行，此生产传统在波斯地区一直持续到了17世纪。然而，中东生产的仿龙泉陶瓷有其自身的缺点。例如，以熔块胎陶为胎体缺少了中国瓷器自身的坚硬度，其釉在使用中也很容易产生刮痕。另外，一些仿龙泉制品的釉在烧造完成后易释放出铅元素，即因铜元素破坏了铅碱釉的稳定性，从而可能使器皿产生毒性。然而，单从视觉效果看，这些中东仿制品代表了当时中东陶瓷化学的创造性胜利。中东陶工通过使用以粉碎的石英和沙漠草木灰为主的配方，颇具技巧地抓住了中国青瓷的特征，并使这类仿制品在广大的地域范围内成功持续生产了几个世纪（本文曾发表于《外国文物里的丝绸之路》，本书略有改动）。

翻译：闻雯　英国牛津大学

致谢：

本文作者衷心感谢闻雯博士将本文从英文翻译至中文；感谢伦敦东方陶瓷协会许可本文使用一些早前发表过的内容；感谢伊恩·弗利斯通教授（Ian Freestone）慷慨提供伦敦大学学院的SEM设备以完成本文所进行的研究；感谢罗莎琳德·韦德·哈登博士（Rosalind Wade-Haddon）提供马穆鲁克陶瓷方面宝贵的专业意见。

注 释

1 Qin Dashu, Chapter 4: Archaeological Investigations of Chinese Ceramics Excavated from Kenya, Selected Works From *Ancient Silk Trade Routes and their influence on Cross Cultural Trade in Asia,* Qin Dashu & Yuan Jian, 87-110.

2 Stevenson J., Guy J., Cort L., *Vietnamese Ceramics: A Separate Tradition,* Chicago, 1997；Sjostrannd S., Turiang: a 14th century Chinese shipwreck, upsetting Southeast Asian ceramic history, *Southeast Asia China Interactions*, ed. Geoff Wade, Royal Asiatic Society.

3 Li Dejin 1994, Technology of Longquan Ware Manufacturing, *New Light on Chinese Yue and Longquan Wares, Archaeological ceramics Found in Eastern and Southern Asia, A.D. 800-1400,* Ho Chuimei, ed., Hong Kong, 1994, 84-99.

4 Impey, O., *The Early Porcelain Kilns of Japan: Arita in the First Half of the Seventeenth Century,* Clarendon Press, Oxford, 1995.

5 *Northeast Asian ceramic interchanges: Korea, China and Japan-the leaders of the World Ceramic History*, Segye Tojagi Eksŭp' o Chojik Wiwŏnhoe, The World Ceramic Exposition, Republic of Korea, 2001；1962 年河北真身舍利塔地基（977 年）就有出土的定窑莲瓣碗，此器形在 10 世纪早期的越窑中也有出现，见张柏主编《中国出土瓷器全集》第 3 册，科学出版社，2008 年。

6 Rawson, J., Tite, M., & Hughes, M., The export of Tang sancai wares: some recent research, *Transactions of the Oriental Ceramic Society 1987-1988*, 52, London 1989, 39-61; Wood, N., Doherty, C., & Rosser-Owen, M. A Technological Study of Iraqi Imitations of Chinese Changsha Wares and Chinese Sancai Wares found at Samarra. *Gu Taoci Kexue Jishu* 7: ISAC' 09, Beijing, 2009, 154-180.

7 Tite, M.S., The technology of glazed Islamic ceramics using data collected by the late Alexander Kaczmarczyk, *Archaeometry 53*, Oxford 2011, 329-339.

8 [日] 佐々木達夫：《中国陶磁器》"アル＝フスタート遺跡 Al Fustat" 第 1 册第 280 ～ 285 页，第 2 册第 435 ～ 487 页，500 ～ 509 页，早稻田大学出版部；Tadanori Yuba, Chinese Ceramics found in al-Fustat Cairo 9th -16th century, *Taoci no. 4*; Revue Annuelle de la Société française d' Étude de la Céramique orientale, Actes du colloque "*Chine-Méditerranée: Routes et éxchanges de la céramique avant le XVI siecle.*" Paris, 2005, 87-93；Tadanori Yuba, Chinese Porcelain found at Fustat based on Research from 1988-2001, *Transactions of the Oriental Ceramic Society,* 76, 2011-2012, London 2013, 1-17.

9 Tadanori Yuba, Chinese Porcelain found at Fustat based on Research from 1988-2001, *Transactions of the Oriental Ceramic Society*, 76, 2011-2012, London 2013, 1-17.

10 同上。

11 Zhao Bing, Chinese-style ceramics in East Africa from the 9th to 16th century: A case of changing value and symbols in the multi-partner global trade, *L'Afrique orientale et l'océan Indien: connexions, réseaux d'échanges et globalisation*, 2015,1-50.

12 Kennet D., Islamic Archaeology in the Gulf, *Hadeeth ad-Dar*, 33, Kuwait, 2011, 28-31.

13 Lin Meicun & Ran Zhang, Zheng He' s voyages to Hormuz: the archaeological evidence, *Antiquity*, 89, 2015, 417-432.

14 Sasaki T., Trade Patterns of Zhejiang Ware found in West Asia, Ho Chuimei ed., *New light on Chinese Yue and Longquan Wares*, Centre of Asian Studies, The University of Hong Kong, 1994, 322-332.

15 Krahl R., Longquan celadon of the Yuan and Ming Dynasties in the Topkapi Saray Museum, Istanbul, *Transactions of the Oriental Ceramic Society*, vol. 49 (1984-1985), London, 1986, 41-57.

16 Synopsis and commentary on a talk by Lim Yah Chiew, "Five Dynasty Treasures: Chinese Ceramics found in the Indonesian Cirebon Shipwreck", *South East Asian Ceramic Society newsletter.* http://www.seaceramic.org.sg/events/synopsis_lyc_lecture18may2010.pdf; Brown R. & Sjorstand. S., *Maritime Archaeology and Shipwreck Ceramics in Malaysia*, National Museum, Kuala Lumpur, Malaysia, 2002.

17 Liebner H. H., *The Siren of Cirebon: A Tenth-Century Trading Vessel Lost in the Java Sea*, PhD thesis, Leeds University, 2014.

18 Sasaki T. & Sasaki H., Arabia hantō ni hirogaru Myanmaa seiji no hakken [Discovery of Myanmar celadon distributed in the Arabian peninsula]. *Kanazawa Daigaku Kōkogaku kiyō (Bulletin of Archaeology, The University of Kanazawa)* 26, Kanazawa, 2002, 1 – 11.

19 National University of Singapore Department of Southeast Asian Studies, *From The Ashes-Reviving Myanmar Celadon Ceramics.*

20 Haddon R.W., *Fourteenth century fine glazed wares produced in the Iranian world, and comparisons with contemporary ones from the Golden Horde and Mamlūk Syria/Egypt*, PhD Thesis. SOAS, University of London, 2011. 英国研究者哈顿曾表示："埃及和叙利亚陶工精于仿制，大量当地制造的仿龙泉青瓷从诸如福斯塔特、亚历山大（Alexandria，埃及）、阿勒颇（Aleppo，叙利亚）和哈马（Hama，叙利亚）等遗址出土，然而，在伊朗出土者却相对较少，也许未来的考古发现会否定这点。"另外，在其博士论文中提到 Takht-I Sulaymān 遗址出土的陶瓷器"提供了充分的证据证明伊朗在伊利汗国时仿青瓷的制造，德黑兰伊斯兰博物馆和柏林博物馆均有相关藏品"。

21 Mason R., & Tite M., The beginnings of Islamic stonepaste technology, *Archaeometry*. 36 (1), Oxford 1994, 77-91; Watson O., *Ceramics from Islamic Lands*,

London, 2004; Haddon R.W., *Fourteenth century fine glazed wares produced in the Iranian world, and comparisons with contemporary ones from the Golden Horde and Mamlūk Syria/Egypt*, PhD Thesis. SOAS, University of London, 2011.

22 Allan J., Abu' lQāsim' s Treatise on Ceramics, *Iran* 11, 1973, 111-120.

23 Mason R., & Tite M., 1994, The beginnings of Islamic stonepaste technology, *Archaeometry*, 36 (1), Oxford 1994, 77-91.

24 Wood N. & Rastelli S., Parallel developments in Chinese porcelain technology in the 13th-14th centuries AD., Chapter 24 in M. Martinón-Torres (Ed.), *Craft and science: International perspectives on archaeological ceramics* (1), Doha, Qatar, 2014.

25 Sundius N. & Steger W., The constitution and manufacture of Chinese ceramics from Sung and earlier times, Section Two of *Sung Sherds* by Nils Palmgren, Nils Sundius & Walter Steger, Stockholm, 1963, 375-505.

26 Paynter S., Links between glazes and glass in mid-2nd millennium BC Mesopotamia and Egypt, *From Mine to Microscope-Advances in the Study of Ancient Technology* (Andrew Shortland, Ian Freestone, Theo Rehren eds.), Oxbow Press, Oxford, 2009, 93-108.

27 Brill R., Some thoughts on the chemistry and technology of Islamic glass, *Glass of the Sultans*(eds. S. Carboni and D. Whitehouse), New Haven and London, 2001, 25-40.

28 同注 22。

29 同注 22。

30 图表左组为本次研究的 9 片马穆鲁克青釉陶瓷片，按照釉层中氧化铅（紫色）含量递增的顺序排列；右组为不同比例组成的钠钙玻璃和铅玻璃混合物，从左至右分别为纯钠钙玻璃、9 份钠钙玻璃与一份铅玻璃、8 份钠钙玻璃与 2 份铅玻璃、7 份钠钙玻璃与 3 份铅玻璃、6 份钠钙玻璃与 4 份铅玻璃、5 份钠钙玻璃与 5 份铅玻璃。马穆鲁克青釉中的铅含量止于 50% 的钠钙玻璃和 50% 的铅玻璃（二硅酸铅）混合后的所显示成分，而多数釉的成分在钠钙玻璃与铅玻璃配比为 6:4 到 5:5 的区间内。

31 Wood N., Doherty C. & Rosser-Owen M., A Technological Study of Iraqi Imitations of Chinese Changsha Wares and Chinese *Sancai* Wares found at Samarra, *Gu Taoci Kexue Jishu 7: ISAC '09,* Beijing, 2009, 154-180.

32 同注 6。

33 Mason R., & Tite M., 1997, The beginnings of tin-opacification of pottery glazes, *Archaeometry*, 39 (1), Oxford, 1997, 41-58; Wood N., & Tite M., Blue and White-the Early Years: Tang China and Abbasid Iraq compared, *Percival David Foundation of Chinese Art Colloquy on Transfer in Chinese Ceramics (Trade, Culture, Technology)*, London, 21-45.

34 同注 31。

35 Vandiver P., & Kingery D., Celadon: The Technological Basis of Their Visual Appearances, Appendix A in *Ice and Green Clouds: Traditions of Chinese Celadon*, Yutaka Mino and Katherine Tsiang eds., Bloomington IN., 1986, 217-224.

36 同注 25。

37 同注 35。

38 Weyl W., *Coloured Glasses*, London, 1959; Bamford C.R., Ionic colouration by transition metals and ligand field theory, *Colour Generation and Control in Glass*, Elsevier Scientific Pub. Co., Amsterdam, 1977.

39 Ishii Tsuneshi, Experiments on the Tenriuji Yellow Celadon Glaze, *Transactions of the British Ceramic Society*, Wedgwood Bi-cenenary Memorial Number, 1930, 352-359.

40 No Hyunggoo, Kim Ungsoo, Kim Jongyoung, et al., Effect of TiO_2 on the color generation in celadon glaze, *Journal of the Korean Ceramic Society*, 2014, 51 (3): 150-155.

41 Pradell T., Molera J., Smith A.D & Tite M.S., The invention of lustre: Iraq 9th and 10th centuries AD, *Journal of Archaeological Science* 35, 2008, 1201-1215.

42 Salinas E., Pradell T., & Molera J., Glaze production at an early Islamic workshop in al-Andalus, *Archaeological and Anthropological Sciences,* 2018; Sasaki T., Trade Patterns of Zhejiang Ware found in West Asia, Ho Chuimei ed., *New light on Chinese Yue and Longquan Wares*, Centre of Asian Studies, The University of Hong Kong, 1994, 322-332.

43 同注 22。

44 Chou Jen, Chang Fu-Kang and Cheng Yung-Fu, Technical Studies on the Lungchuan Celadons of Successive Dynasties, *Khao-ku Hsu eh-pao*, 1, 1973, 131-156.

45 同注 22。

46 Allan J., Abu' l Qāsim' s Treatise on Ceramics, *Iran* 11, 1973, 111-120; Chou Jen, Chang Fu-Kang and Cheng Yung-Fu, Technical Studies on the Lungchuan Celadons of Successive Dynasties, *Khao-ku Hsu eh-pao*, 1, 1973, 131-156.

47 Slinn G., Health and safety in ceramic education-glazes, *Artisan, the Podmore Craft Pottery Newsletter*, 7, Stoke-on-Trent, 1-6.

48 Harris R. & Elsea W., Ceramic glaze as a source of lead poisoning, *Journal of the American Medical Association*, 202(6), 1967, 544-546.

49 Wood N., *Chinese Glazes: Their Chemistry, Origins and Re-creation.*, A & C Black Ltd. and University of Pennsylvania Press, 1999.

The Manufacture of Longquan Celadon Re-creations in Islamic Lands

Nigel Wood, University of Westminster, UK, School of Archaeology, University of Oxford, UK
Chris Doherty, School of Archaeology, University of Oxford, UK

The imitation of imported Chinese Longquan celadon wares in the Middle East is a significant if somewhat neglected aspect of Islamic ceramic history. Building on centuries of experience in recreating imported Chinese wares with local materials, Islamic potters of the thirteenth to the seventeenth century CE produced their own versions of Longquan celadon wares – rather as potters in South East and East Asia were achieving at the same time. Middle Eastern potters however, faced unique challenges as they worked with earthenware materials and oxidised firings, and had little or no knowledge of the original Chinese techniques. Through the adoption of stonepaste bodies and often with the modification of tin-opacified glazes they produced convincing local versions of the Chinese originals. Skilful blending of iron, copper and (sometimes) cobalt oxide colourants allowed them to match the glaze-colours of Longquan wares with some precision, and the glazes were also applied thickly, in the Longquan manner. Compositionally, the glazes fall within the alkali-lime glass to lead-eutectic 'system', and the heat-work applied can be proposed as equivalent to about Orton Cone 06 – typically circa 1000°C.

In terms of abundance, it now seems likely that locally made Longquan imitations were popular in the Middle East from the thirteenth to the fifteenth centuries CE, and that the tradition continued in Persia well into the seventeenth century. However, the Middle Eastern Longquan imitations did have some drawbacks. For example the stonepaste material lacked the toughness of the original Chinese wares, and the earthenware glazes would have scratched easily in use. There is also some likelihood that the imitated Longquan glazes were disposed to lead-release after firing, due to the de-stablising effect of copper in lead-alkali glazes. However, from the purely visual perspective, these wares represent a triumph of creative ceramic chemistry. Through the use of recipes based largely on crushed quartz and the ashes of desert plants the potters of the Middle East captured the qualities of the Chinese originals with great skill, and also managed their production on a considerable scale for many centuries, and over an extensive geographical area.

中国青瓷对日本陶瓷的影响

[日] 森达也　冲绳县立艺术大学

自古以来，中国陶瓷对日本陶瓷的发展有着强烈的影响。中国青瓷一直是日本陶瓷生产模仿的对象，尤其是龙泉青瓷，甚至可以称为日本人最喜爱的中国陶瓷。

日本陶瓷生产初期的技术并不成熟，产品独具风味，直至17世纪才开始正式生产青瓷，江户时期日本青瓷已可以精湛地模仿明代的龙泉青瓷。

8世纪以后，中国的陶瓷大量输出至日本，且被作为高级日用器而受到贵族、僧侣和武士等阶层青睐。被运送到日本的中国陶瓷当中，虽有唐三彩、青瓷、白瓷、黑釉瓷、褐釉瓷、青花瓷、五彩瓷等诸多种类，但其中数量较多的还是龙泉青瓷。不仅如此，这些龙泉青瓷还对同时代的日本陶瓷产生了强烈的影响。

本文旨在对日本陶瓷简史、输入日本的中国青瓷情况以及龙泉窑等中国青瓷对日本陶瓷产生的影响进行简单归纳论述。

一　窑火初生：远古时期至奈良、平安时代的日本陶器

在日本，目前公认的最早的陶器是公元前14500年前后制作的无釉陶（绳文陶器）。日本的无釉陶（在日本被称为“土器”）是通过露天烧（不用窑，而是覆以柴草烧成的方法）在700℃～900℃左右的温度下烧制而成的。这类烧成技术从绳文时代（公元前14500年到公元前1000年左右）起，历经弥生时代（公元前1000年左右到公元3世纪中期）直至古坟时代前期（3世纪后半期到4世纪）的约15000年间，基本没有太大变化。

（一）硬陶的传入

在4世纪末、5世纪初期前后（古坟时代），从朝鲜半岛南部东渡到日本的陶工带来了烧制灰色硬陶的技术，使用原始的龙窑（日本称之为“窖窑”）在1100℃左右的温度下烧制而成，于是日本终于正式开始了烧窑业。这种硬陶烧制技术起源于中国江南地区的印纹硬陶烧制技术。

这一时期的硬陶在日本被称为“须惠器”（图1）。须惠器的产地最初以大阪南部和九州北部为中心，在之后的大约100年间，其产地遍布于自日本东北地区到南部九州地区的大面积区域。早期的须惠器与朝鲜半岛南部的硬陶（在韩国称之为“硬质土器”）在品种和器形上极其类似。但自7世纪前后，须惠器中模仿自中国和朝鲜半岛进口的响铜（用辘轳车加工的、器壁被切削甚薄的青铜器）器形的产品增多，这些日本独特的产品有异于朝鲜半岛产品，从而成为主流。

图1　7世纪　须惠器长颈瓶
日本爱知县陶磁美术馆藏

图2　6世纪　白釉绿彩连珠纹碗残件
日本长崎县壱岐双六古坟出土
日本长崎县教育委员会藏

图3　9世纪　猿投窑绿釉炉
日本爱知县陶磁美术馆藏

图4　五代　越窑青釉碗
故宫博物院藏

（二）铅釉与灰釉

在日本，陶瓷器的施釉始于7世纪后半期（飞鸟时代），从朝鲜半岛传入的低温烧成铅釉技术带动了日本绿釉陶的生产。到了8世纪奈良时代（710～794年），在当时的都城——平城京（今奈良）周边，有模仿唐三彩烧制的三彩陶瓷，被称为奈良三彩。长崎县壱岐（即壹岐岛）双六古坟出土的6世纪中后期的北朝白釉绿彩连珠纹碗[1]（图2）和奈良石上神社出土的绿釉连珠纹碗被认为是日本出土的中国陶瓷中年代最为古老的。其后，在日本各地的寺院和古墓中相继发掘出土了7世纪末期至8世纪前期的唐三彩。从日本施釉陶器在产生之初绿釉和三彩陶瓷就得以生产这一点来看，应该能够反映出该阶段传入日本的中国陶瓷中多以铅釉陶器为主[2]。

奈良三彩采用了绿釉、褐釉、白釉（透明釉）三种颜色的釉料，其生产一直持续到8世纪末，到了9世纪（平安时代），褐釉已不见踪迹，绿釉陶器的生产成为主流。9世纪以后的绿釉陶瓷产地迁移到山口、京都及其周边、爱知县北部（包括岐阜东南部）三个地区，其中爱知县的猿投窑作为绿釉陶器的生产中心而不断发展。在猿投窑开始生产铅釉绿陶器的同时，还开始生产灰釉陶器——施有以植物灰烬为主要原料的灰釉，而后在1200℃左右高温下烧制而成。虽然该类产品在日本被称之为"陶器"，但其烧成温度和施釉的情况与中国的原始青瓷相似，从与中国陶瓷的比较来看，猿投窑的灰釉陶器也可以被认为是日本瓷器的起源[3]。

图5　9世纪　猿投窑灰釉执壶
日本爱知县陶磁美术馆藏

（三）越窑青瓷的影响

9～10世纪猿投窑所生产的绿釉陶器的器形和品种被广泛认为是受到了越窑青瓷的影响。这一时期猿投窑生产了很多模仿越窑青瓷的玉璧底碗、托、香炉（图3）、盒、香炉、查斗（唾壶）、划花纹碗、执壶（水注）、有盖双耳壶、四足壶等产品。其生产的灰釉陶器中也有不少模仿越窑青瓷的玉璧底碗（图4）、执壶（图5、图6）、四足壶等产品。

9～10世纪，越窑青瓷、邢窑白瓷、长沙窑陶瓷、巩义窑白瓷、唐三彩和福建怀安窑的粗制青瓷等产品，在当时日本九州北部的博多（今福冈市）大宰府（当时掌管日本与中国及朝鲜外交与贸易的机构所在地）、京都（即当时的都城平安京）以及各地的寺院和官府遗址中都有出土。这些出土的中国陶瓷中，数量最多的就是越窑青瓷，此时期对日本陶瓷影响最大的也是越窑青瓷。

猿投窑生产的仿越窑青瓷绿釉和灰釉陶器是当时日本最上乘的陶瓷器，其上供至日本中央政府之后，再被作为官用品分配至全国各地的官府、寺院。

图6　宋　越窑青釉执壶
故宫博物院藏

图 7　11 世纪晚期　猿投窑灰釉花口碗
日本爱知县陶磁美术馆藏

图 8　12 世纪晚期　福建青釉栉目纹碗
日本爱知县陶磁美术馆藏

图 9　14 世纪 濑户窑灰釉三足炉
日本爱知县陶磁美术馆藏

图 10　明早期　龙泉窑青釉三足炉
故宫博物院藏

（四）“珠光青瓷”与龙泉青瓷的初现

猿投窑的绿釉陶器生产于 11 世纪左右结束，12 世纪主要生产灰釉陶器，其中有不少模仿当时大量传入日本的福建白瓷碗和青瓷碗、碟等器形的产品（图 7）。12 世纪后半期被运至日本的福建产栉目纹青瓷（图 8），由于为室町时代茶师村田珠光所珍藏，因此被称为“珠光青瓷”。龙泉青瓷传入日本也在该时期，而且在当时作为对华贸易据点的九州博多和首都京都等地都出土了少量 11 世纪末到 12 世纪初的龙泉青瓷。12 世纪末开始，龙泉窑青釉碗、碟则被大量运送至日本。

图 11　15 世纪　濑户窑灰釉尊形瓶
日本爱知县陶磁美术馆藏

二　风貌独特：镰仓时代到安土桃山时代的日本陶瓷器

（一）另辟蹊径的模仿

12 世纪末，继承了猿投窑灰釉技术的濑户窑在爱知县濑户地区开窑，之后历经镰仓时代（1192 年左右至 1333 年）、室町时代（1336 ～ 1573 年）和安土桃山时代（1573 ～ 1603 年），逐渐繁荣并发展成为日本最上乘陶瓷的产地。

濑户窑仿造生产了龙泉青瓷，景德镇青白瓷，福建青瓷、白瓷和建盏，江西赣州窑小壶（茶叶罐）等产品。虽然当时濑户窑已仿照龙泉青瓷的式样生产制作出了鬲式炉（袴腰香炉）（图 9、图 10）、尊形瓶（图 11、图 12）、酒会壶（盖罐）（图 13）、盘（图 14 ～图 16）、花瓶（图 17、图 18）等器物，但仅凭借当时的灰釉陶（原始青瓷）技术，尚无法做出完美的仿造品，因此当时濑户窑的工匠们在器形和纹样上独辟蹊径，从而造就了与龙泉青瓷有着迥异质感和风格的产品。

濑户窑的产品从镰仓时代到室町时代，作为日本产的最上乘的陶瓷器，在当时被赋予仅次于中国陶瓷的地位。这一时期的濑户窑陶瓷，除了在镰仓时代的政治中心——镰仓大量出土以外，在日本全境的武士的大型房子遗址、古城遗址、寺院遗址等地相继被发现，从而可以判断出它受到了当时的武士和僧侣们的喜爱并在当时的日本全国流通。

图 12　明早中期　龙泉窑青釉鼓钉纹觚　故宫博物院藏

（二）龙泉青瓷传入日本的全盛时期

13 ～ 14 世纪，被大量运至日本的中国陶瓷（包括龙泉青瓷，景德镇青白瓷，福建青瓷、白瓷、黑釉瓷）以龙泉窑青瓷的数量最多（图 19），特别是南宋后期龙泉窑所生产的高档粉青釉瓷在日本尤为珍贵，在室町时代后期到桃山时代深受茶师们喜爱。到了江户时代（1630 ～ 1868 年），这类高档龙泉青瓷被称为“砧青瓷”（图 20）。砧是用来把布变柔软的木制工具，其形状很像一类龙泉窑青瓷瓶，因而产生了“砧青瓷”的叫法。还有一种说法是，在茶道上大有成就的千利休所拥有的一件青瓷花瓶出现了裂纹，“裂纹”（ひび Hibi）一词和砧木敲击时发出的响声（響き Hibiki）在日语中的发音几乎是一致的，因而由这种谐音诞生出了“砧青瓷”的叫法。在日本有大量南宋砧青瓷名品流传至今，被

图 13　14 世纪　濑户窑灰釉酒会壶（罐）
大阪市立东洋陶磁美术馆所藏

图 14　15 世纪　濑户窑灰釉四足盘
日本爱知县陶磁美术馆藏

图 15　14 世纪　濑户窑灰釉鱼纹盘
日本爱知县陶磁美术馆藏

图 16　北宋　龙泉窑青釉刻鱼纹折腰盘
故宫博物院藏

图 17　14 世纪　濑户窑灰釉双环耳瓶

图 18　明早期　龙泉窑青釉双环耳瓶
故宫博物院藏

图 19　13 世纪后期　龙泉青瓷
日本镰仓今小路西遗址出土
日本镰仓市教育委员会藏

图20　13世纪　龙泉窑“砧青瓷”凤耳瓶
日本大阪市立东洋陶磁美术馆藏

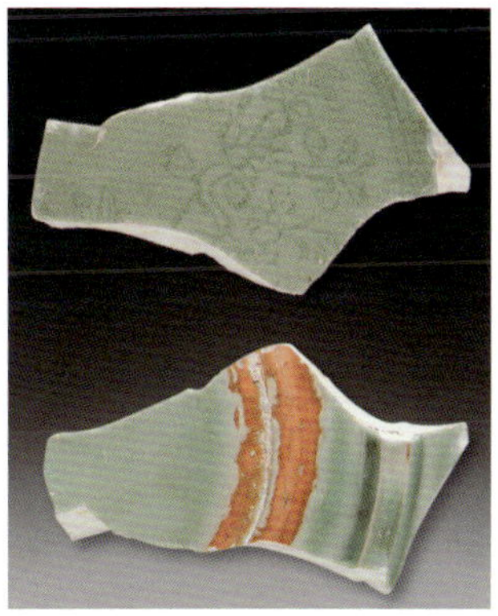

图 21　明　龙泉窑青釉刻松竹梅纹盘残件
日本那霸市渡地遗址出土
日本冲绳县埋藏文化财中心藏

各寺院、官府、大名家以及茶师们的后人一直传用。而元代至明代初期所生产的龙泉青瓷，由被称作“大龙寺船”的日本贸易船运到日本，因此被称为“天龙寺青瓷”。在这个龙泉窑青瓷传入日本的全盛时期，濑户窑对龙泉青瓷的仿造也达到了顶峰。

14 世纪后半期到 15 世纪，传入日本的中国陶瓷仍以龙泉青瓷为主，同时还有景德镇窑的白瓷、青花瓷以及福建的白瓷、黑釉瓷（天目瓷）等，但由于受到明朝海禁政策的影响，被带到日本的中国陶瓷总体数量较之前减少了。与明王朝结成册封关系的琉球王国（今冲绳）在该时期进口了数量庞大的龙泉青瓷、景德镇青白瓷和福建陶瓷，通过转运贸易再销往日本、东南亚、朝鲜半岛。通过考古发掘，在冲绳本岛的今归仁古城、首里城和渡地遗址（那霸港口遗址）出土了少量的明早期龙泉窑官器（图 21 ~ 图 23），这些官器应该是明朝皇帝赐给琉球王的赏赐品。

这一时期，虽然濑户窑仍在继续仿造以龙泉窑青瓷为代表的中国陶瓷，但多用朴素的印花纹和铁釉（黑釉、褐釉）等独特装饰，同时增强其独特的色彩感，产品风貌与中国的青瓷、白瓷在质感上的差距也越来越大。

时至战国时代（1493～1573 年），濑户窑和濑户附近的美浓窑继续仿造以碗、碟等小型器物为主的中国青瓷，而且以施微黄色厚重灰釉的产品居多（图 24）。

图 22　明早期　龙泉窑青釉刻划折枝花果纹执壶
故宫博物院藏

图 23　明早期　龙泉窑青釉印花团龙纹绶带耳葫芦式扁瓶
故宫博物院藏

图 24　15 世纪　濑户窑灰釉碟残件
日本爱知县陶磁美术馆藏

图 25　16~17 世纪
“七官青瓷”鱼耳瓶
日本爱知县陶磁美术馆藏

（三）龙泉青瓷被替代

到了 16 世纪，进入日本的中国陶瓷变为以景德镇青花瓷为主流，青瓷则以 16 世纪初期为分界点数量锐减。日本进口的青瓷中也几乎不再是龙泉青瓷，而是以景德镇窑青瓷占据主体地位。16 世纪末到 17 世纪前半叶，被带到日本的青瓷被称之为“七官青瓷”（图 25），其中一部分被认为是与“古染付（青花）”（图 26、图 27）等一起由日本向中国订购的。虽然“七官青瓷”以往多被视为龙泉青瓷，但笔者认为，实际上很可能多数都是在景德镇窑生产的仿龙泉青瓷。

图 26　17 世纪　“古染付”三足盘（景德镇民窑产品）
日本爱知县陶磁美术馆藏

图 27　明宣德　景德镇窑青釉刻划花卉纹菱花口折腰碟
故宫博物院藏

三　优质青瓷的产生：江户时代的日本陶瓷

进入 17 世纪，运送到日本的中国陶瓷大多为景德镇窑青花瓷器以及福建漳州窑的青花瓷器（图 28）和五彩瓷器，青瓷仅能看到前述被称为七官青瓷的景德镇窑仿龙泉窑青瓷和漳州窑青瓷。

江户时代（1603 ~ 1868 年）早期濑户窑和美浓窑还生产仿龙泉青瓷的陶瓷器（图 29、图 30）。17 世纪初，随着来自朝鲜半岛的陶瓷烧造技术的传播，日本真正开始烧造瓷器的历史，在九州有田窑及其邻近的波佐见窑中，模仿烧造明代龙泉窑青釉盘、碗逐渐得以实现（图 31、图 32）。有田窑和波佐见窑的主要产品是仿景德镇窑的青花瓷器（图 33），但在 17 世纪也有不少青瓷产品。佐贺县的锅岛藩开创了被称为日本官窑的锅岛藩窑，在生产上等青花瓷器和五彩瓷器的同时，还生产出了优质青瓷（被称之为锅岛青瓷）（图 34、图 35），且倍受喜爱。

江户时代中期到后期，诞生于九州的日本瓷器技术传播到以京都、濑户为代表的日本各地，并在生产青花和五彩瓷的同时，逐渐开始生产青瓷（图 36、图 37）。

在京都，青木木米（1767 ~ 1833 年）和钦古堂龟祐（1765 ~ 1837 年）以青瓷名家而闻名，特别是钦古堂龟祐，他除了向在兵库地区进行高档青瓷生产的三田窑（图 38）传授青瓷技术外，还向兵库地区的王地山窑及和歌山地区的男山窑等日本西部地区推广青瓷生产技术。从江户时代中期到后期，以京都为中心的关西地区所生产的青瓷以模仿明代龙泉青瓷釉色的产品居多，即主要生产“梅子青”釉青瓷。

图 28　16 世纪末至 17 世纪初　漳州窑青花开光盘
日本爱知县陶磁美术馆藏

图 29　17 世纪　褐釉琮式瓶
日本爱知县陶磁美术馆藏

图 30　明　龙泉窑青釉琮式瓶
故宫博物院藏

图 31　17 世纪　有田窑青釉刻花叶纹盘
日本爱知县陶磁美术馆藏

图 32　明早期　龙泉窑青釉刻折枝牡丹纹折沿盘
故宫博物院藏

图 33　17 世纪　有田窑青花舟纹盘
日本爱知县陶磁美术馆藏

图 34　18 世纪　锅岛藩窑青釉盘
日本爱知县陶磁美术馆藏

图 35　明早期　龙泉窑青釉盘　故宫博物院藏

日本正式的青瓷生产始于 17 世纪，在此之前的 9 世纪到 16 世纪末，通过铅釉陶和灰釉技术模仿来自中国的越窑青瓷、龙泉青瓷、福建产青瓷的器形和纹样。由于当时日本仿造高档中国青瓷的技术并不成熟，因此其质感与中国陶瓷有着很大的差异，但是通过独特的器形设计与纹饰运用，其风格与作为标榜的中国陶瓷相比极为迥异，从而开创了日本仿造青瓷的新境界。

17 世纪以后，日本首先在九州的有田窑和波佐见窑开始生产青瓷，到了 18、19 世纪，以京都为中心的关西地区开始生产出上乘的青瓷，由此也可清晰看出明代的龙泉窑青瓷对江户时期日本青瓷的影响（本文曾发表于《外国文物里的丝绸之路》，本书略有改动）。

翻译：胡一超　景德镇陶瓷大学

图 36　17 世纪　濑户窑青釉手桶形水指（提梁桶形水罐）
大桥秋二烧造
日本爱知县陶磁美术馆藏

图 37　明　龙泉窑青釉提梁桶
故宫博物院藏

图 38　19 世纪　三田窑青釉鸭形盒
钦古堂龟祐烧造
日本爱知县陶磁美术馆藏

注 释

1 [日] 弓场纪知 :《壱岐双六古坟出土の白釉緑彩円文碗—その年代と中国陶磁史上での位置づけ—》,《双六古坟》长崎县壱岐市教育委员会, 2006 年。

2 也有青瓷的传入, 传世品中有奈良法隆寺青瓷盘口双耳壶 (6 世纪后半期至 7 世纪初福建烧造), 由此可以得知在当时已有青瓷传入日本。

3 学界普遍认为日本的瓷器起源于 17 世纪初在有田开始生产的白瓷和青花瓷。

参考文献

1 [日] 井上喜久男 :《尾张陶磁》, ニューサイエンス社 , 1992 年。

2 [日] 井上喜久男 :《日本の三彩と与绿釉》, 爱知县陶磁资料馆 , 1998 年。

3 [日] 森达也 :《明时代后期の中国陶磁と日本陶磁への影响》,《桃山陶の华丽な世界》第 50 ~ 52 页, 爱知县陶磁资料馆 , 2005 年。

Influences of Chinese Celadon Upon Japanese Ceramics

MORI Tatsuya, Okinawa Prefectural University of Arts

Chinese ceramics had exerted strong influences upon the development of ceramics in Japan since very long time ago. In particular, celadon from China had always been the object of imitation in production of Japanese ceramics. Celadon from the Longquan kilns could especially be considered the most beloved Chinese ceramics in Japan.

From the end of the 12th century onward, celadon bowls and dishes from the Longquan kilns were exported to Japan in large quantities. The Seto ware kilns that inherited the ash glaze techniques of the Sanage kilns started to fire objects in forms copying Longquan celadon. However, they greatly differ from Longquan celadon in terms of texture, quality and style. From the late 14th century to the 15th century, Chinese ceramics exported to Japan decreased in overall quantity, and Japan obtained Longquan celadon through the Ryukyu Kingdom. Products from the Seto kilns increasingly differed from celadon and white porcelain from China in terms of texture and quality. During the Sengoku period (Age of Warring States, c. 1493-1573), the Seto ware kilns and Mino ware kilns nearby continued to copy Chinese celadon. Most of these are small vessels like bowls and dishes, and are usually thick and heavy with yellowish ash glaze. Starting in the early 16th century, celadon from Longquan kilns exported to Japan decreased dramatically, and porcelain with celadon glaze from Jingdezhen kilns in Jiangxi occupied the main position. In the early 17th century, with the spreading of ceramic techniques from the Korean Peninsula, Japan started to fire real celadon. During the middle to late Edo period, the Kansai region centred around Kyoto produced celadon and most of these copied the glaze colour of Ming dynasty Longquan celadon, i.e., the 'plum-green' glaze.

清宫旧藏景德镇仿龙泉青瓷的历史地位及与龙泉青瓷的比较研究

董健丽　故宫博物院

龙泉窑是浙江省著名的青瓷窑址，位于龙泉市境内，创烧于北宋早期[1]，南宋晚期是它的极盛时期，至明中期以后逐渐走向衰落。龙泉青瓷以其纯美葱翠的釉色、优良的质地、精美的花纹和丰富的造型博得人们的喜爱，是我国古代青釉发展的高峰，产品销往全国各地，甚至到海外，对国内众多瓷窑乃至东南亚、中东地区的陶瓷生产都产生重要影响，自宋代以后的各朝仿品层出不穷，成为国内外众多瓷窑的仿烧对象，宋、元、明、清各时代均有仿制，浙江、福建、广东、江西、湖南等省都有仿烧龙泉青瓷的窑口，特别是明、清景德镇御窑厂的烧造水平达到了历史的顶峰。

一　故宫博物院藏明代景德镇仿龙泉青瓷

明代景德镇在元代制瓷基础上，逐渐鹤立鸡群，入明后已是独领风骚，居全国制瓷业的盟主地位，尤其是明中期后，随着各大窑场的衰落，形成了景德镇“工匠来八方，器成天下走”的局面。青花、斗彩以及多种多样的高低温釉器风靡一时，包括龙泉窑在内的全国其他各窑都望尘莫及。据史料记载，洪武二年明朝宫廷开始在江西景德镇设置御窑厂，并选派特定人员对皇家御用瓷器的烧造事务专门管理，主事人员由中央派员或是地方官员督陶管理等[2]。御窑厂更是汇集了全国各地最优秀的能工巧匠，占据最优质的制瓷原料，按照宫廷样式，不计工本，烧造出大量的精美瓷器，既有本朝创新品种，又有模仿名窑瓷器的仿古瓷，其中仿龙泉青瓷就是著名品种。景德镇仿龙泉青瓷，又称“仿龙泉”，是以浙江龙泉窑器的青釉为模仿对象，用紫金釉微掺青料合成，根据釉色深浅不同定名有豆青、冬青（东青、冻青）、翠青、粉青等，其中以豆青色最重，釉色深且浓，釉质肥腴；冬青次之，色调匀净苍翠，釉面平整光润；粉青最浅，釉色淡，釉质细匀，以上都属于青釉瓷器，具有仿宋代龙泉青瓷的效果[3]。

对景德镇珠山御窑遗址的发掘证明，永乐时期有仿龙泉青瓷，宣德时期御窑厂开始大量烧造仿龙泉青瓷[4]。关于宫廷使用的景德镇永乐、宣德时期仿龙泉青瓷见于北京毛家湾瓷器坑出土的资料[5]。毛家湾位于明代皇城的西北，与皇城仅一墙之隔，且坑内出土有171件仿龙泉青瓷，其中永乐至宣德时期的光素撇口碗、鸟食罐、钵形炉、带系筒形壶、高足杯等，皆为白胎，釉色青绿，釉面匀净光洁，制作精细，为御窑所烧，笔者认为这批仿龙泉青瓷是为宫廷烧造的，见有明永宣青釉碗（图1）、明永宣青釉壶（图2）、明中期青釉月华纹菱花口盘（图3）等。

到嘉靖时期，御器厂每年的烧造任务中已有大量的仿龙泉青瓷，据《江西大志》记载，嘉靖二十二年烧造“青碗二千、青盘一千、青碟二千、青靶盅一千、青瓷茶盅二千、青酒盏一万”，嘉靖二十三年“烧成桌器一千三百四十桌，每桌计二十七件，内案酒碟五、果碟五、菜碟五、碗五、盖碟三、茶盅、酒盏、渣斗、醋注各一”。在这1340件桌器中就有“翠青色一百六十桌”[6]，可见明代宫廷已把景德镇御窑厂作为生产翠青釉的基地，直接为宫廷服务。同时，景

图 1　明永乐至宣德　青釉碗残件
北京毛家湾明代瓷器坑出土

图 2　明永乐至宣德　青釉壶残件
北京毛家湾明代瓷器坑出土

图 3　明中期　青釉月华纹菱花口盘残件
北京毛家湾明代瓷器坑出土

图 4　明永乐　翠青釉三系盖罐
故宫博物院藏

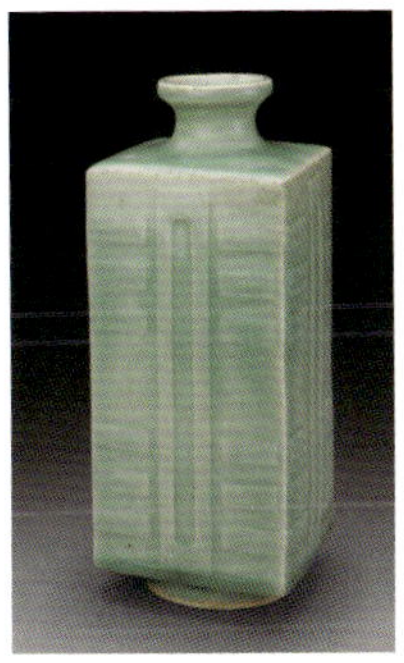

图 5　明永乐　翠青釉八卦纹琮式瓶
故宫博物院藏

图 6　明宣德　冬青釉葵口盘
故宫博物院藏

图 7　明宣德　豆青釉划花菱花口折腰碟
故宫博物院藏

图 8　明嘉靖　青釉暗划花直口瓶
故宫博物院藏

德镇的仿龙泉青瓷亦进入贵族和权贵的生活中，如明益宣王朱翊鈏夫妇合葬墓[7]、明益定王朱由木墓[8]、江西境内明刑部尚书魏源墓[9]等都出土了仿龙泉青瓷珍品。

除上述出土品外，故宫博物院收藏的明代仿龙泉青瓷共计 15 件，釉色有粉青、冬青、豆青、翠青等，从明代初年延续到明代晚期，按时代先后顺序划分：

永乐时期有 6 件，分别是：粉青釉刻花碗、豆青釉划花缠枝莲纹碗、翠青釉盘、冬青釉高足碗、翠青釉三系盖罐（图 4）、翠青釉八卦琮式瓶（图 5）等，釉色有粉青、淡青、翠青、豆青等釉色，器物多光素，见少量的暗划花装饰。釉色青中闪绿，苍翠欲滴；釉质肥厚，多小气泡及垂流现象，也偶有匀净无气泡的；施釉均匀，釉面玻璃质强，口边釉薄处闪白，并且微露胎骨[10]。

宣德时期有 3 件，分别是：宣德款冬青釉葵口盘（图 6）、宣德款豆青釉划花菱花口折腰碟（图 7）、淡青釉蟋蟀罐，釉色青翠透亮，温润似玉。釉面匀净，釉质莹润无气泡。釉色深者青翠，玻璃质感较强；浅者如新鲜之青豆色，十分雅静。有缠枝莲和缠枝灵芝纹等暗花装饰[11]。

嘉靖时期有 3 件，分别是：嘉靖款青釉暗划花直口瓶（图 8）、冬青釉镂空笔山、“永保长春”款青釉暗花四方罐（图 9），其青绿色调介于豆青和粉青釉之间，釉面肥厚，光亮洁净，玻璃质强，纹饰有暗刻灵芝和竹纹等。

万历时期有 4 件，分别是：万历仿宣德款豆青釉划花菱花口折腰碟（图 10）、玉堂佳器款冬青釉暗刻云龙纹三足炉、玉堂佳器款豆青釉三足钵式炉、冬青釉狮形水盛等。万

图 9　明嘉靖　“永保长春”款青釉暗花四方罐
故宫博物院藏

图 10　明万历　仿宣德款豆青釉划花菱花口折腰碟
故宫博物院藏

图11　清康熙　豆青釉暗花缠枝牡丹纹花觚
故宫博物院藏

图12　清康熙　豆青釉划花缠枝花纹笔筒
故宫博物院藏

图13　清雍正　粉青釉鬲式炉
故宫博物院藏

历时期景德镇仿龙泉青瓷的釉色较嘉靖朝色调浅淡，泛黄白色，造型不太规整，款字略显潦草，万历仿龙泉青瓷除署“大明万历年制”款或“大明宣德年制”仿款外，还见有民窑产品署“玉堂佳器”等吉言赞颂款。

上述故宫博物院藏景德镇仿龙泉青瓷以官窑产品为主，亦不乏民窑精品，造型多种多样，按功能分有日常用器、文房用品、陈设品和雕塑品等，如日常生活中的盘、碗、洗等，文具中的笔山、水盛等，陈设用品中的琮式瓶、三足炉等，其中尤以仿宋代的龙泉窑琮式瓶最为精致。这些器物胎体洁白，质地细腻，采用刻花、划花、镂雕等装饰手法，器物多有本朝款，时代涵盖了从明初到明晚期的产品，弥补了出土资料的不足，其洁白的胎体，莹润的釉色，精细的制作，使其价值高于同期的龙泉窑青瓷产品。

二　故宫博物院藏清代景德镇仿龙泉青瓷

清代初期景德镇御窑厂管理因袭前朝旧制，并随着烧造事务的不断增多，开始派遣内务府官员驻场督造，如康熙时期的臧应选、郎廷极，雍正至乾隆时期的年希尧、唐英，他们对清代御窑瓷器的烧造起了举足轻重的作用。由于雍正、乾隆皇帝对瓷器嗜古成癖，致使清代仿古之风盛行，尤其是对宋代瓷器的仿制更是风靡一时，雍正时期督陶官唐英《陶成纪事碑记》中记载当时在其“岁例供御”中就有57种釉彩之多，其中就有仿龙泉釉深浅两种[12]。清代仿龙泉青瓷体现在两个方面，一方面仿宋代龙泉窑流行的粉青、冬青、梅子青和仿古器形鼎、炉、尊等，另一方面仿明代的豆绿釉和刻花工艺。

（一）故宫博物院藏清代景德镇仿龙泉釉青瓷的特征

从故宫博物院现存实物看，清代仿龙泉釉青瓷，其烧造年代自康熙开始至宣统结束，以康熙、雍正、乾隆时期数量最多，约有500余件，其中既有官窑制品，也有民窑器物，以官窑器为大宗，且制品最精，代表了清代仿龙泉青瓷的最高水平。

康熙时期仿龙泉青瓷共计35件，有日用器、陈设器、文房用具等，如碗、盘、瓶、花觚（图11）、笔筒（图12）等，其中笔筒的数量最多，梅瓶、花觚、直颈瓶、缠枝莲纹大盘、菱花口盘、卧足碗等延续着传统造型，以仿龙泉青瓷造型为主，所用纹饰多采用刻划花工艺，有缠枝牡丹纹、缠枝莲纹、蕉叶纹、如意云纹、夔龙纹、双螭衔灵芝纹、山水、水波纹等。款识多为本朝款，同时亦有少量的仿前朝款。

雍正时期仿龙泉青瓷共计24件，有碗、高足碗、盘、瓶、花觚、炉、笔筒等，釉色有豆青、粉青和冬青等，器物多书本朝款，所仿的南宋龙泉窑青釉斗笠碗、八方贯耳瓶、鬲式炉等，仿造水平极高，特别是粉青釉鬲式炉（图13），几乎到了以假乱真的程度。雍正时期景德镇仿龙泉青瓷，整体造型一改康熙时期坚硬挺拔的风格，代之为精致秀雅之风貌，器物造型既仿前朝龙泉青瓷，亦新创器形，其中摹古之作，几可乱真。如：玉壶春瓶，仿明初龙泉窑青釉玉壶春瓶式样和纹饰；鬲式炉，从造型和釉色上完全仿南宋龙泉窑青瓷产品；葫芦瓶，仿南宋龙泉窑制品，在此基础上创新出上圆下方的葫芦形瓶。仿品从造型、釉色、装饰技法以及底足处理上与真品极为相近，但不可避免地带有本朝釉面光亮、胎质洁白、器形规整的时代特征。创新之作，有四连瓶、洗口瓶、八方瓶、扁肚瓶、瓜棱蒜头瓶、石榴尊、络子尊、花口尊、三系壶、直口瓶、鼓式罐、五孔方瓶、花插、花盆等。器物在外形处理上含蓄柔和，没有急剧的转折，表现为一种连贯流畅的起伏状，具有鲜明的时代特征。仿龙泉窑青釉见有冬青釉、粉青釉、豆青釉，每种釉色之中还有深浅不同的变化，豆青釉色则多仿明龙泉窑釉色，釉色或青中带黄，或青釉浓重呈橄榄色，釉面肥腴，多书本朝款识，有“大清雍正年制”“雍正年制”六字或四字篆书及楷书款，其书写形式有6种，这也是在雍正官窑瓷器中，款识书写形式较多的一个品种。

乾隆时期景德镇仿龙泉釉青瓷共计446件，有碗、碟、盘、洗、瓶、罐、花觚、尊、炉、笔筒等，有日用器、陈设器、文房用具等，其中以各种瓶的数量最多，表明这时期的仿龙泉青瓷是以陈设器为主。釉色有豆青、粉青、冬青等釉色，以本朝款为主，所仿明代龙泉窑青釉菱花口碟、刻花梅瓶（图14）、壮罐（图15）、琮式瓶等与真品神似，所不同的是质量更好。本朝造型除少量沿用传统的琮式瓶、梅瓶、贯耳瓶、胆瓶、玉壶春瓶、花觚、兽耳瓶、葫芦形瓶、花口盘等传统龙泉青瓷造型之外，大多延续了雍正时期的样式，但不及雍正朝秀美，总体风格与雍正朝相近，造型除日常所用盘、碗、碟之外，开始大量烧造瓶、尊、炉等琢器，器形更富于变化，釉色以冬青、粉青釉为多见，器物通体施青釉，底足边际显露淡淡的黄色，装饰工艺除传统的刻、划、印之外，镂雕工艺开始大量出现，装饰内容更加丰富，寓意吉祥的图案盛行，纹饰题材有缠枝花纹、蕉叶纹、石榴纹、云蝠灵芝纹、海水云龙纹、八宝夔纹、弦纹、八卦纹、福字等，圆形器外底有圆形支钉痕迹，采用支烧方法，器物款识有"大清乾隆年制""乾隆年制"六字、四字青花篆书款及刻款，少量器物不署款识。

纵观故宫博物院藏的清代康熙、雍正、乾隆时期景德镇仿龙泉青瓷，藏品数量多，种类齐全，造型规整，釉色丰富，纹饰精细，代表了青瓷烧造的最高境界，虽然仿效龙泉青瓷，但两者在釉色、造型、纹饰、烧造方法等方面有很大区别。

图14　清乾隆　豆青釉刻缠枝牡丹纹梅瓶
故宫博物院藏

图15　清乾隆　豆青釉凸花云龙纹带盖壮罐
故宫博物院藏

（二）清代景德镇仿龙泉青瓷的功用和使用场所

对于故宫博物院旧藏的清代景德镇仿龙泉釉青瓷其功用和使用场所是需要进一步探讨的问题，《清宫瓷器档案全集》[13]有了较全面的揭示：

1．供奉之器

雍正、乾隆时期的仿龙泉青瓷菱花口碟、高足盘（靶盘）、高足碗（靶碗）、盖罐为祭祀用器，供奉于宗教祭祀场所，见下列档案记载：

雍正二年，太监总管张起麟交佛前供的豆绿瓷靶碗九件。

乾隆十二年，佛堂供器：冬青釉菱花式三寸碟一百件、冬青釉菱花式二寸五分碟一百件。

乾隆二十一年，乾隆佛堂收冬青釉靶盘十件、冬青釉葵花式靶碗五件。

乾隆四十一年，佛日楼供冬青釉菱花式碟四十五件。

乾隆四十三年，佛堂收冬青釉菱花式二寸五分碟五十五件。佛日楼供冬青釉菱花式碟四十五件。

乾隆四十五九月十九日宗镜大昭之庙供器：冬青釉盖罐。

由此可知，各种规格的冬青釉菱花式碟、冬青釉靶盘（高足盘）、冬青釉靶碗（高足盘）、冬青釉盖罐作为供器，在宫廷内的祭祀场所使用。

2．插花陈设用具

雍正豆青釉双系尊、双管瓶、蒜头瓶等的用途在档案中也有记载：

雍正八年，太监范国用持来豆青瓷双喜樽一件，传旨，着配一紫檀木座，瓶内安寿意花一束。

雍正十二年，宫殿监李英交豆青瓷双管瓶一对，传旨，着配做通草拱花一对，再将一统樽式炉送进一件来。

雍正十三年，太监交冬青蒜头瓶一件，传旨，俱各配象牙花，无座者，配座。

可知豆青双喜樽（双系尊）、豆青双管瓶、冬青蒜头瓶用作插花陈设，对于插何种花，亦有明确规定，如"寿意花""通草拱花""象牙花"等。

3．做饮食用器

关于康熙、雍正、乾隆时期大量仿龙泉釉青瓷碗、高足碗、盘、渣斗等使用场所见下面档案记载：

乾隆四十一年，御膳房旧存：雍正款豆青靶碗五件、豆青靶盘八件、豆青五寸瓷碗九十件、豆青磬口大碗二件、豆青大碗一件、豆青五寸墩子碗一件、豆青大铙碗一件、豆青暗花碗一件、豆青暗花莲子碗一件。

乾隆五十八年，御膳房现存旧窑瓷器：康熙款豆青五寸盘七件、豆青大碗一件、豆青铙碗一件、豆青莲花碗七件、豆青墩子五寸碗七件、豆青五寸盘三十件、豆青五寸靶碗一件。雍正年制豆青渣斗二件、一尺一寸东青拱花碗五件、八寸东青拱花碗三十件、七寸东青拱如意碗十七件。乾隆年制东青釉瓷罐二件。

上述各类碗、高足碗、盘、渣斗等存放在御膳房，御膳房是清朝掌管宫内备办饮食以及典礼筵宴所用酒席等事物的机构，由此推断，上述瓷器为宫中饮食宴饮用具，并多以豆青釉为主。

由此可见，故宫博物院藏清代景德镇仿龙泉釉青瓷用于宫廷的陈设、祭祀、宴饮等宫廷生活中，为帝王所享用。

（三）雍正、乾隆帝与仿龙泉青瓷

故宫博物院藏清代仿龙泉釉青瓷在宫中有很高的地位，被帝王所青睐，清代帝王基于其汉文化的修养，不仅接受汉人的审美，对于汉人烧造的器物，大加仿制，喜爱备至，如雍正、乾隆帝对仿宋代龙泉青瓷十分关注，倾注着很多情感，对仿龙泉青瓷，也做了很多细致具体的工作，如对器物配座、配盖、擦洗、刻字分等级等。还对器物进行改造，具体对器物配何种花及摆放何处等很多细节都亲自过问。此外，还将龙泉釉青瓷赏赐给督府大员，见下列档案记载：

（1）配匣：雍正六年，太监胡全忠交来仿龙泉窑三线瓶一件，传旨，着配一杉木匣盛装[14]。

（2）配盖：乾隆三年五月初六日，太监高玉交龙泉釉二件……传旨，着交唐英俱配瓷盖[15]。

（3）改造：乾隆三年，太监高玉交龙泉釉糖锣洗一件。传旨，着将糖锣洗交与唐英照此釉水烧造，另改花样……[16]

（4）擦洗、分等级：乾隆九年，太监胡世杰交来龙泉釉海棠式水盛一件（随铜匙）传旨着认看等次。太监胡世杰交来龙泉釉暗花双耳纸槌瓶一件、龙泉釉戟耳炉一件，传旨，擦洗送进[17]。

（5）刻字分等级：乾隆二十四年，太监交冬青鸡式熏炉一件，传旨配座，刻三等，太监交冬青鹭鸶熏炉一对，传旨，配香几，呈样得时在静宜园学古堂地平上摆[18]。

（6）规定摆放地点：乾隆二十四年，太监交冬青鹭鸶熏炉一对，传旨，配香几，呈样得时在静宜园学古堂地平上摆[19]。

（7）器物配花：雍正八年，太监范国用持来豆青瓷双喜樽一件，传旨，着配一紫檀木座，瓶内安寿意花一束[20]。雍正十二年，宫殿监李英交豆青瓷双管瓶一对，传旨，着配做通草拱花一对，再将一统樽式炉送进一件来[21]。雍正十三年，太监交冬青蒜头瓶一件，传旨，俱各配象牙花，无座者，配座[22]。

（8）赏赐：雍正七年，太监胡全忠交来豆青瓷瓶一件，赏总督鄂尔泰[23]。雍正八年，太监范国用持来豆青瓷双喜樽一件，传旨，着配一紫檀木座，瓶内安寿意花一束。太监李文明持来豆青瓷笔洗一件，豆青宝月瓶一件，赏云贵总督鄂尔泰[24]。

综上所述，我们对故宫博物院藏清代景德镇仿龙泉釉青瓷的入宫时间、藏品数量、种类、用途、使用场所、雍正、乾隆二帝对龙泉釉青瓷的关注等，有了更多的认知。

三　景德镇仿龙泉青瓷与浙江龙泉青瓷的比较研究

（一）明代景德镇仿龙泉青瓷与龙泉青瓷的区别

明代龙泉地区生产的青瓷，称之为龙泉中心窑区产品，其特征主要是胎质细腻，胎色灰白，釉色滋润，釉层较厚，器物绝大多数内外满施青釉，唯外底足有一周涩圈，露胎处泛火石红色。器形规整，质量较高，属于尖端产品。明代景德镇仿龙泉釉青瓷除了仿龙泉青瓷的釉色、造型外，与龙泉青瓷在胎、釉、烧造工艺等方面有很大差异，下面以故宫博物院藏品为例，进行对比研究：

（1）故宫博物院藏明永乐翠青釉高足碗（图16）：口径16厘米，足径4.7厘米，高11.3厘米。高足碗造型轻盈秀美，

图 16　明永乐　翠青釉高足碗
故宫博物院藏

图 17　明早期　青釉印金刚杵纹高足碗
龙泉大窑枫洞岩窑址出土

图 18　明宣德　豆青釉菱花口折腰碟
故宫博物院藏

图 19　明中期　龙泉窑青釉划花菱花口折腰碟残件
龙泉大窑枫洞岩窑址出土

高足作竹节式，通体青釉，光素无纹，釉质温润，色泽匀净，是一件难得的仿烧龙泉青瓷代表作品。该器与龙泉大窑枫洞岩窑址出土明龙泉窑青釉印金刚杵纹高足碗比较（图 17）[25]，釉色青翠，胎体轻薄，制作精良。

（2）故宫博物院藏明宣德豆青釉菱花口折腰碟（图 18）：口径 8.8 厘米，足径 4.1 厘米，高 3 厘米。碟敞口，折腰，圈足，口作菱花瓣式。通体施豆青色釉，釉层肥厚，有开片。器里外刻划暗花纹，近足处有蕉叶纹。碟内心青花楷书“大明宣德年制”六字双行款，该器釉色朦胧浅淡，与龙泉大窑枫洞岩窑址出土明中期龙泉窑青釉划花菱花口折腰碟的区别是内底有青花款（图 19）[26]。

通过对比可见，明代景德镇仿龙泉青瓷与浙江产龙泉青瓷存在的差异，表现为：

（1）胎体不同。明代景德镇仿龙泉青瓷胎骨略轻，胎体洁白细腻，制作较为精细。明代浙江龙泉青瓷胎体厚重，质地坚密，颜色为灰白色。

（2）釉色不同。明代景德镇仿龙泉青瓷釉层略薄，釉色清淡，有开片。清末许之衡《饮流斋说瓷》载：“明仿龙泉，与宋无甚大异，唯其色略淡、其釉略薄耳。”[27] 在釉色为贵的问题上，宋人和明人审美观念、鉴赏标准不同，宋人重粉青色，而明人则重翠青（豆青）色[28]。明代龙泉青瓷釉层较厚，釉色深浓，以青绿为主，也有浅黄、淡绿、绿褐等色。

（3）烧造方法不同。明代景德镇仿龙泉青瓷采用垫饼垫烧而成，足端刮釉。底足削刮工艺规整精细，有的器物在底足或器里署本朝款识。明代龙泉青瓷碗盘类器物均采用裹足支烧法，外底挂釉形成涩圈，露胎处泛火石红色。

明代仿景德镇龙泉青瓷，特别是官窑器，大多密藏清宫，胎体洁白，质地细腻，釉色莹润，器物多属本朝款，其精良的制作，代表了明代景德镇仿龙泉青瓷的最高水平，与浙江龙泉青瓷有很大的区别，其价值高于同期的龙泉青瓷产品。

（二）清康熙、雍正、乾隆时期景德镇仿龙泉青瓷与龙泉青瓷的区别

这时期的仿龙泉青瓷主要仿宋、明两朝的龙泉青瓷，仿宋代器物有碗、洗、炉、觚、琮式瓶、胆瓶、贯耳瓶、双耳瓶、兽耳瓶和凤尾尊等，仿明代者有碗、高足碗、盘、梅瓶、执壶、笔筒等。清三代的仿龙泉青瓷从造型、釉色、纹饰、烧造方法上多方面仿烧龙泉青瓷。同时具有本朝特征，下面从以下几个方面进行剖析解读：

（1）釉色、造型和纹饰模仿龙泉青瓷。故宫博物院藏雍正时期景德镇烧造的冬青釉斗笠盏、青釉玉壶春瓶和粉青釉鬲式炉等，与龙泉青瓷相比，形神兼备，几可乱真。两者的差别是仿品釉面洁白，釉色莹润，底足处理更加规整，带有雍正朝官窑瓷器的典型特征。如故宫博物院藏雍正粉青釉鬲式炉（见图 13），从釉色和造型两方面仿南宋龙泉窑青釉鬲式炉，与故宫博物院藏南宋龙泉窑青釉鬲式炉虽然极为相近（图 20），但器形较宋器略大，底足制作较为精细，具有清雍正时期瓷器十分精致的时代特征。

图20　南宋　龙泉窑青釉鬲式炉
故宫博物院藏

图21　清雍正　粉青釉暗花蕉叶纹觚
故宫博物院藏

图22　南宋　龙泉窑青釉觚
日本东京国立博物馆藏

图23　明永乐　龙泉窑青釉刻花梅瓶
故宫博物院藏

（2）造型和纹饰大致模仿龙泉青瓷。故宫博物院藏雍正、乾隆时期景德镇生产的仿龙泉窑青釉簋式炉、缠枝花樽式炉、凸弦纹樽式炉、凤尾尊和暗花蕉叶纹觚等，与龙泉窑同类器物比较，造型和纹饰上大致相同，只不过清代仿品比较小巧，纹饰上有所添加。如故宫博物院藏清雍正粉青釉暗花蕉叶纹觚（图21），器物清秀，与日本东京国立博物馆藏南宋龙泉窑青釉觚（图22）[29]相比，没有龙泉青瓷器腹丰满，亦无出脊装饰，显得更庄重古朴，仿青铜器意味更浓厚。

（3）造型仿龙泉青瓷，但外底烧造方法迥异。清代景德镇仿龙泉青瓷蒜头瓶、梅瓶、刻花盘造型与龙泉青瓷同类器物极为神似，不仅仿造型，也仿明代的刻花工艺，但装烧工艺与龙泉青瓷却有天壤之别，器外底涩胎无釉，举例如下：

清乾隆仿龙泉豆青釉刻缠枝牡丹纹梅瓶（见图14），此器不仅仿明代龙泉青瓷造型，也仿刻花工艺，但外底涩胎无釉，而明代龙泉青瓷则外底满釉，足端挂釉（图23）。

清雍正仿龙泉青釉暗划缠枝花纹折沿盘（图24），此器仿明代龙泉青瓷的刻花装饰，外底涂褐色，而明代龙泉青瓷则裹足支烧，外底有垫烧留下的一周火石红，内有青釉（图25），外底的处理方式有很大区别。

（4）造型仿龙泉青瓷，但署本朝年款。这类器物最大特点是仿龙泉青瓷的造型，有的器物仿的十分逼真，如清雍正款冬青釉六角贯耳瓶、乾隆款冬青釉八卦纹琮式瓶等，这类器物与宋代龙泉青瓷同类器物几乎完全一样，只是外底署本朝款识，雍正朝所仿器物有篆书和楷书两种，而乾隆所仿器物多用篆书，盘类圆器款识写在器物内底，而琢器类款识则写在器外底，有青花款和刻款两种，举例如下：

故宫博物院藏清雍正款粉青釉菊瓣纹折沿盘（图26），此盘釉色粉青，外底施白釉，青花双圈内书“大清雍正年制”六字楷书款，此盘仿明代龙泉窑青釉菊瓣纹菱花口折沿盘的造型（图27）[30]。真品外底不施白釉，裹足支烧，且无款识。

故宫博物院藏清乾隆豆青釉凸花云龙纹带盖壮罐（见图15、图28），此器造型和釉色仿明代龙泉青瓷同类器，外底有“大清乾隆年制”四字篆书款，而明代龙泉青瓷器物外底有一周火石红（图29）。

纵观康熙、雍正和乾隆时期的仿龙泉青瓷，康熙时期的仿龙泉青瓷从造型和釉色两方面仿制，口沿和底足的处理方式为本朝特点，所仿器物器形伟岸雄浑，胎质坚细，釉面光滑细腻，胎釉结合紧密，纹饰上极力追求仿古铜器的效果。雍正的仿龙泉青瓷有的器物在造型、釉色、底足的处理方式几乎完全仿造，造型纤细秀丽，器形比例协调，有所谓的“曲线美”，釉面有橘皮纹是其突出特征，采用刻、印、划、堆塑等工艺手法美化瓷器，仿古造型多，仿造水平极高。乾隆时期仿龙泉釉青瓷造型端庄规整，大小器物制作均很精致。

图 24　清雍正　青釉暗划缠枝花纹折沿盘底部
故宫博物院藏

图 25　明　龙泉窑青釉印折枝西番莲纹盘底部
故宫博物院藏

图 26　清雍正　粉青釉菊瓣纹折沿盘
故宫博物院藏

图 27　明早中期　龙泉窑青釉菊瓣纹菱花口折沿盘
日本出光美术馆藏

图 28　清乾隆　豆青釉凸花云龙纹壮罐外底
故宫博物院藏

图 29　明永乐　龙泉窑青釉印折枝莲纹带盖壮罐
故宫博物院藏

结语

龙泉青瓷以其纯美葱翠的釉色、优良的质地和多种造型及精美的花纹博得人们的喜爱，为我国古代青釉发展的高峰，对中国南方广大区域的瓷窑和东南亚一些国家的瓷器产生了很大的影响。尤其是对江西景德镇的陶瓷生产影响深远，自明永乐、宣德时期开始，景德镇御器厂烧制大量仿龙泉青瓷，成为宫廷仿烧龙泉青瓷的基地，同时，景德镇丽阳乡瓷器山明代瓷窑址的发掘表明，景德镇民窑场在宣德时期已大量生产龙泉青瓷[31]。随着景德镇官窑、民窑仿烧龙泉青瓷的不断增加，强大的竞争使龙泉青瓷逐渐从宫廷用瓷的生产基地中退出，生产规模逐渐缩小并逐步走向衰落。景德镇仿龙泉青瓷的质量与浙江龙泉青瓷不相上下，或略胜一筹，景德镇御窑厂秉承皇帝的旨意，用的是当时最好的原料、窑工，所烧造的仿龙泉青瓷质量甚至超过同时期的龙泉窑产品，产品胎质洁白细腻，釉色品种丰富，釉面柔和清澈，犹如美玉一般的华润丰盈，其造型更是典雅不失端庄，秀巧更具妩媚，成为清代瓷器造型之典范。清代景德镇仿龙泉青瓷渗透到了宫廷生活的方方面面，在宫中有很高的历史地位，表现了清帝对汉文化的推崇和吸收。明清景德镇仿龙泉青瓷逐渐摆脱了龙泉青瓷的束缚，逐渐形成各种新的拓展，于清代达到顶峰，明清景德镇仿龙泉青瓷至今不断地影响着中国现代设计，成为中国工艺美术和现代设计的重要特色，在青瓷烧造历史上占有一席之地。

注 释

1 中国硅酸盐学会：《中国陶瓷史》第 274 页，文物出版社，1982 年。

2 王光尧：《清代御窑厂的管理与生产制度》，《中国古代官窑制度》，紫禁城出版社，2004 年。

3 耿宝昌：《明清瓷器鉴定》上册第 166 页，中国文物商店总店，1983 年。

4 北京大学考古文博学院：《江西景德镇明清御窑遗址发掘报告》，《文物》2007 年第 5 期。

5 北京市文物研究所：《毛家湾明代瓷器坑考古发掘报告》（下）第 308 页，科学出版社，2007 年。

6 （明）王宗沐：《江西大志》卷七“陶书 · 供御”。

7 江西省文物工作队：《江西南城明益宣王朱翊鈏夫妇合葬墓》，《文物》1982 年第 8 期。

8 江西省文物工作队：《江西省南城明益定王朱由木墓发掘简报》，《文物》1983 年第 2 期。

9 余家栋：《江西玉山、临川和永修县明墓》，《考古》1973 年第 5 期。

10 同注 3，第 32 页。

11 同注 3，第 55 页。

12 （清）唐英：《陶成纪事碑记》，《唐英集》，辽沈书社，1991 年。

13 铁源、李国荣：《清宫瓷器档案全集》，中国画报出版社，2008 年。

14 同上，卷一第 92 页。

15 同上，卷一第 295 页。

16 同上，卷一第 295 页。

17 同上，卷二第 254 页。

18 同上，卷四第 151 页。

19 同上，卷四第 151 页。

20 同上，卷一第 135 页。

21 同上，卷二第 201 页。

22 同上，卷一第 246 页。

23 同上，卷一第 119 页。

24 同上，卷一第 136 页。

25 浙江省文物考古研究所、北京大学考古文博学院、龙泉青瓷博物馆：《龙泉大窑枫洞岩窑址出土瓷器》第 176 页，文物出版社，2009 年 5 月。

26 同上，第 220 页。

27 （清）许之衡：《饮流斋说瓷》“说窑第二”，邓宝辑《美术丛书》三集第六辑。

28 明陆容《菽园杂记》：“凡绿豆色莹净无暇者为上，生菜者次之。”明高濂《遵生八笺》：“定窑之下龙泉次之……今则上品仅有葱色，余尽油青色矣。”

29 ［日］爱知县陶磁资料馆：《龙泉窑青磁展》第 41 页，日本爱知县陶磁资料馆，2012 年。

30 同上，第 80 页。

31 故宫博物院等：《江西景德镇丽阳瓷器山明代窑址发掘简报》，《文物》2007 年第 3 期。

Ming-Qing Period Porcelain with Longquan-Style Celadon Glaze from the Qing Court Collection: Their Significance and Comparison with Celadon from the Longquan Kilns

Dong Jianli, the Palace Museum

In the collection of the Palace Museum are large number of Ming-Qing period Jingdezhen porcelain with celadon glaze imitating Longquan wares. A deep systematic research on this type of porcelain has been lacking for a long period of time. Based on information from essential literature, such as *Archive on Display Items in the Qing Imperial Palace, Report of Taking Stock of Objects in the Former Forbidden City* (1925), *Qing Dynasty Archive of Various Workshops of Office of Manufacture, Department of Imperial Household Affairs,* and *List of Tribute Items for the Imperial Palace,* this article investigates a variety of issues related to this group of porcelain. These include their names, characteristics, origins, status and usage inside the palace, and the impact of personal taste of Qing emperors on their production and use.

The research also compares and differentiates porcelain with Longquan-style celadon glaze made in Jingdezhen, Jiangxi with celadon wares made in Longquan, Zhejiang. It provides useful reference materials for correct differentiation and identification of celadon wares made in kilns of Longquan, proper Longquan style celadon made in other kilns, and inferior imitation of Longquan wares made in provincial kilns. The research also provides a useful standard for reliable dating of related objects.

龙泉大窑青瓷釉色特征

故宫博物院　浙江省文物考古研究所　龙泉市博物馆

引言

龙泉窑位于浙江省龙泉市境内，从窑址遗存的标本可以看出，南宋晚期是龙泉窑的极盛期，元代在烧大件器物的技术上有所突破，明中期以后逐渐走向衰落[1]。我国烧造青瓷的历史十分久远，青瓷釉色与质地之美的顶峰即是宋代窑工创造的龙泉青瓷，它是巧夺天工的人工制造的青玉，每一块宋代龙泉青瓷碎片，至今仍令我们为它的釉色所倾倒[2]。

按照窑址的地域分布，龙泉窑可分为东区和南区两大部分，其中以龙泉南区为核心，而龙泉南区又以大窑为核心[3]。明代陆容所著《菽园杂记》中即记载："青瓷初出于刘田，去县六十里，次则有金村窑，与刘田相去五里余……然泥油精细，模范端巧，俱不若刘田。"文中的"刘田"即是大窑。

为配合故宫博物院"天下龙泉——龙泉青瓷与全球化"展览，本文采用分光光度计、光学显微镜、X 射线荧光能谱仪等现代科学分析仪器，对龙泉大窑出土的不同时期青瓷釉层进行分析研究，以期揭示龙泉大窑青瓷釉色特征。

一　样品与测试方法

（一）样品

本文分析的龙泉大窑瓷片包括叶坞底（YWD）、岙底（AD）、枫洞岩（FDY）三个遗址，其中叶坞底样品时代为南宋晚期，岙底和枫洞岩样品时代涉及元代和明代。所有瓷片样品釉面皆为青釉，胎均为灰胎，典型样品如图所示（图1）。

（二）测试方法

采用美国 X-Rite 公司的 Color i5 分光光度计对样品表面进行颜色测试，选取干净平滑的釉面区域，测量光谱范围为 400nm~700nm。

采用美国 EDAX 公司生产的 Eagle III XXL 微聚焦型能量色散 X 射线荧光光谱分析仪测试样品的化学成分，束斑直径 300μm，电压 25kV，电流 600μA，测试时间 300s，采用自建的定量曲线算出样品的定量分析结果。

采用德国 Leica 公司的 DM4000 型偏光显微镜进行岩相显微结构分析，将瓷片断面粘于玻璃片上后磨制成厚度为 30μm 的光薄片。

YWD-20 叶坞底南宋时期青瓷样品

YWD-29 叶坞底南宋时期青瓷样品

AD-2 岙底元代时期青瓷样品

AD-6 岙底元代时期青瓷样品

AD-86 岙底明初青瓷样品

FDY-44 枫洞岩元代时期青瓷样品

FDY-2 枫洞岩明初青瓷样品

图1 龙泉大窑出土的青瓷样品

二 龙泉大窑青瓷釉色测试结果

从样品照片中可以看出不同窑厂不同时代所产青瓷的釉色存在着一定差异。为了科学表征龙泉大窑青瓷釉层的颜色，建立起时代、样品类型与釉层颜色的对应关系，本文选择了有代表性的93片样品进行了颜色测试，所有结果列于表1中。LCH为色彩空间，其中L为明度，标准黑的L接近0，标准白的L为100。C和H是色度坐标，C为饱和度，即颜色点与原点的距离；H为色相，即颜色点与原点连线的角度。

表1 龙泉窑瓷片釉层颜色色度值

编号	年代	L	C	H	编号	年代	L	C	H
YWD-2	南宋	54.6	9.5	160.9	YWD-13	南宋	63.39	6.45	158.8
YWD-3	南宋	65.6	6.46	141.6	YWD-14	南宋	62.35	6.12	144.4
YWD-8	南宋	67.48	7.67	136.6	YWD-16	南宋	59.14	8.92	134.5
YWD-9	南宋	51.39	9.68	128.2	YWD-17	南宋	54.9	8.28	132.3
YWD-11	南宋	62.53	7.95	145.6	YWD-18	南宋	64.96	6.44	137.2
YWD-12	南宋	57.11	7.14	145	YWD-20	南宋	54.69	11.77	135.1

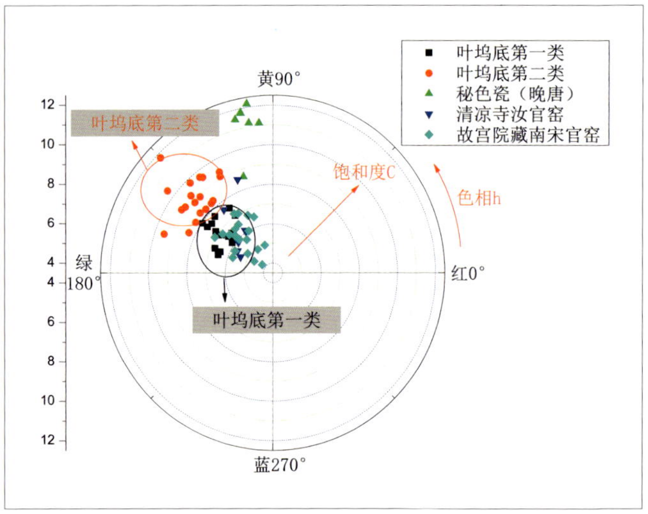

图 2　不同类型青瓷釉色 CH 色度图

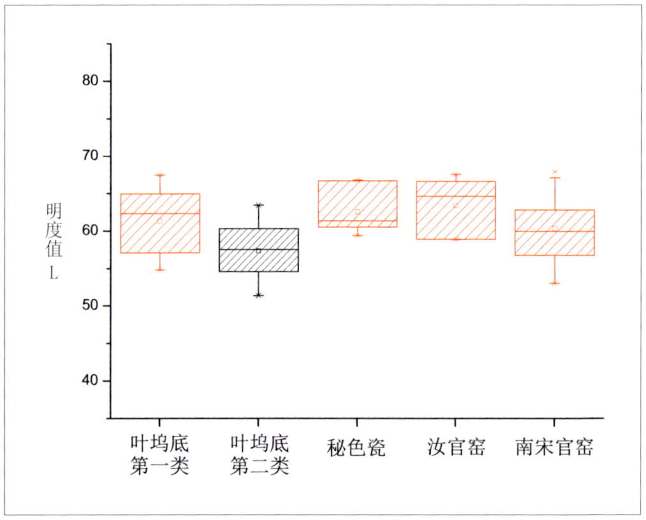

图 3　叶坞底两类样品釉色明度值 L 箱式图

续表 1

YWD-22	南宋	65.45	6.77	157.7	AD-44	元	54.04	11.65	117.5
YWD-27	南宋	62.56	9.12	119.5	AD-49	元	54.09	14.14	108.9
YWD-28	南宋	55.52	7.5	124.7	AD-51	元	66.43	6.66	149.3
YWD-29	南宋	59.89	6.37	139.6	AD-52	元	55.79	8.51	151.4
YWD-30	南宋	58.36	8.27	137.3	AD-53	元	49.18	13.08	110.6
YWD-32	南宋	58.98	8.33	155.1	AD-54	元	51.66	12.26	107.2
YWD-34	南宋	52.9	9.33	118.7	AD-56	元	55.06	13.08	113.5
YWD-37	南宋	61.59	6.5	162.3	AD-62	元	57.01	16.78	99.67
YWD-38	南宋	57.54	8.32	130.5	AD-64	元	48.97	13.99	97.4
YWD-43	南宋	58.2	9.16	143.8	AD-65	元	58.37	12.62	115.4
YWD-45	南宋	54.84	7.02	124	AD-66	元	60.1	11.16	128.5
YWD-46	南宋	60.32	8.92	138.7	AD-68	元	54	13.16	112.4
YWD-47	南宋	60.25	7.55	142	AD-69	元	53.68	8.73	144.9
YWD-49	南宋	60.44	8.28	147.5	AD-70	元	58.32	14.7	108.9
YWD-55	南宋	63.46	9.58	127.1	AD-72	元	56.71	8.32	146.2
YWD-56	南宋	54.3	9.78	133.4	AD-73	元	59.14	7.84	136.6
YWD-57	南宋	52.73	8.37	141.3	AD-75	元	58.54	8.44	141.1
YWD-58	南宋	57.06	10.39	142.8	AD-80	明初	53.23	14.19	118.5
YWD-59	南宋	60.93	9.24	146	AD-81	明初	55.35	13.95	119
YWD-63	南宋	55.48	7.64	145.7	AD-82	明初	58.81	12.8	120.4
YWD-64	南宋	63.65	6.8	144.6	AD-84	明初	54.45	10.53	122.1
YWD-74	南宋	57.45	9.3	137.5	AD-85	明初	48.28	14.13	116.2
AD-1	元	59.25	10.11	145.1	AD-86	明初	56.21	13.33	109.5
AD-2	元	62.76	9.35	140.1	AD-87	明初	54.05	12.91	123.8
AD-3	元	61.95	8.93	136.3	FDY-2	明初	57.69	13.4	106.2
AD-4	元	61.83	12.61	126.3	FDY-4	明初	41.47	12.13	93.35
AD-6	元	57.7	14.2	109	FDY-5	明初	49.78	12.48	109.2
AD-11	元	53.02	12.18	110.6	FDY-7	明初	49.48	13.06	105.1
AD-12	元	43.78	14.59	109.5	FDY-9	明初	53.34	12.96	100.6
AD-13	元	55.48	14.74	114.1	FDY-10	明初	54.61	13.08	97.47
AD-14	元	54.57	11.54	126.4	FDY-11	元	54.43	15.45	99.87
AD-16	元	52.1	12.26	120.1	FDY-17	元	57.75	10.81	118.7
AD-22	元	52.72	12.53	107.3	FDY-25	元	54.24	14.11	102.7
AD-23	元	54.34	13.1	111.9	FDY-27	元	53.18	12.45	111.8
AD-26	元	54.37	12.02	104.6	FDY-34	元	53.62	10.79	107.6
AD-28	元	54.82	10.45	106.7	FDY-35	元	48.95	15.67	97.77
AD-29	元	52.39	13.42	115.5	FDY-42	元	51.65	13.22	112.6
AD-32	元	47.42	13.54	117.5	FDY-44	元	48.3	9.81	125.7
AD-33	元	45.76	13.77	106.9	FDY-48	元	56.11	12.19	111.1
AD-39	元	48.04	12.28	101.1	FDY-57	元	53.02	14.51	110.4
AD-43	元	51.35	12.55	112.5					

三　龙泉大窑不同时期青瓷釉色分析与讨论

（一）南宋时期釉色分析结果与讨论

南宋时期是龙泉青瓷发展的鼎盛时期[4]，为了探寻南宋龙泉青瓷在中国青瓷釉色发展过程中的地位、唐宋时期中国青瓷釉色发展规律，本文将唐宋时期以青瓷釉色著称的另外三个窑厂的产品——越窑秘色青瓷[5]、北宋清凉寺汝官窑青瓷、南宋官窑青瓷[6]的典型样品的釉面颜色与南宋龙泉叶坞底青瓷釉色共同画入色度图中以做比较（图2）。图中反映了样本釉面的色相H和饱和度C值，色相即色彩的相貌，饱和度反映了色彩的鲜艳程度。从图中可以看出，唐宋时期中国著名青瓷窑产品的釉色有一定的共性，即色度坐标基本处于黄绿区域内，但不同时期、不同窑厂的样品釉色又具有不同的特点。

晚唐时期越窑秘色青瓷釉色的色相角较小，位于第二象限靠近90° 黄色轴附近，同时饱和度值很高，故古诗中形容秘色瓷釉色的“千峰翠色”应该属于视觉效果为饱和度较高且较青黄的釉色。中国青瓷发展到北宋时期，由于釉料配方及烧制工艺的改进，出现了清凉寺汝官窑青瓷“雨过天青云破处”的天青釉色，相较于唐代秘色瓷，汝窑釉色的色相角更大，即更偏青，同时饱和度大大降低。南宋时期的浙江青瓷发展非常繁荣，其中官窑中最有代表性的即是南宋官窑，其釉色色度值与北宋汝窑相近，均属于色相角较大（135° 附近）、饱和度较低（平均值为6）的青瓷釉色。

从色度坐标上来看，龙泉大窑叶坞底青瓷釉面颜色可分为两类，其中第一类样品色相角平均值在140° 左右，饱和度值在7左右，与北宋汝窑青瓷和南宋官窑青瓷均相近，釉色呈较为淡雅的粉青色。南宋时期龙泉窑有一部分产品被供应到宫廷和贵族[7]，叶坞底第一类样品的釉色便有可能为此类。第二类叶坞底青瓷釉面色相角与第一类叶坞底、北宋汝窑、南宋官窑接近，但其饱和度值明显偏高（均值在9以上）。饱和度即是颜色的鲜艳程度，低饱和度的颜色显得不太鲜艳，但却十分耐看、雅致和沉稳，而高饱和度的颜色虽然显得非常鲜艳和活泼，可在短时间内吸引到人的目光，但却非常容易引起人的视觉疲劳。第二类叶坞底青瓷釉色稍显艳丽，无法达到当时南宋宫廷审美标准，故这一部分龙泉青瓷可能为满足普通百姓市场的需要而烧制。此外，从明度值箱式图中还可看出（图3），叶坞底第一类、秘色瓷、汝官窑和南宋官窑青瓷的明度值均较高，而叶坞底第二类青瓷釉色明度值稍低，故中国唐代晚期至南宋时期的宫廷对青瓷釉色的审美倾向于稍低饱和度、稍高明度的青色。

（二）元明时期釉色分析结果与讨论

南宋后期是龙泉窑发展的鼎盛时期，元明时期是龙泉窑青瓷制作开始衰退的时期[8]。为了对比南宋后期和元明时期的龙泉大窑青瓷釉色、从颜色角度分析龙泉窑后期衰退的原因，本文将南宋叶坞底、元明岙底、元明枫洞岩出土青瓷残片釉色的CH值画入色度图中（图4）。

从图中可以看出，元代岙底窑产品釉色可分为两类，其中第一类产品色相角较大（平均值在140° 左右），饱和度较低（平均值在8左右），均与叶坞底南宋时期釉色接

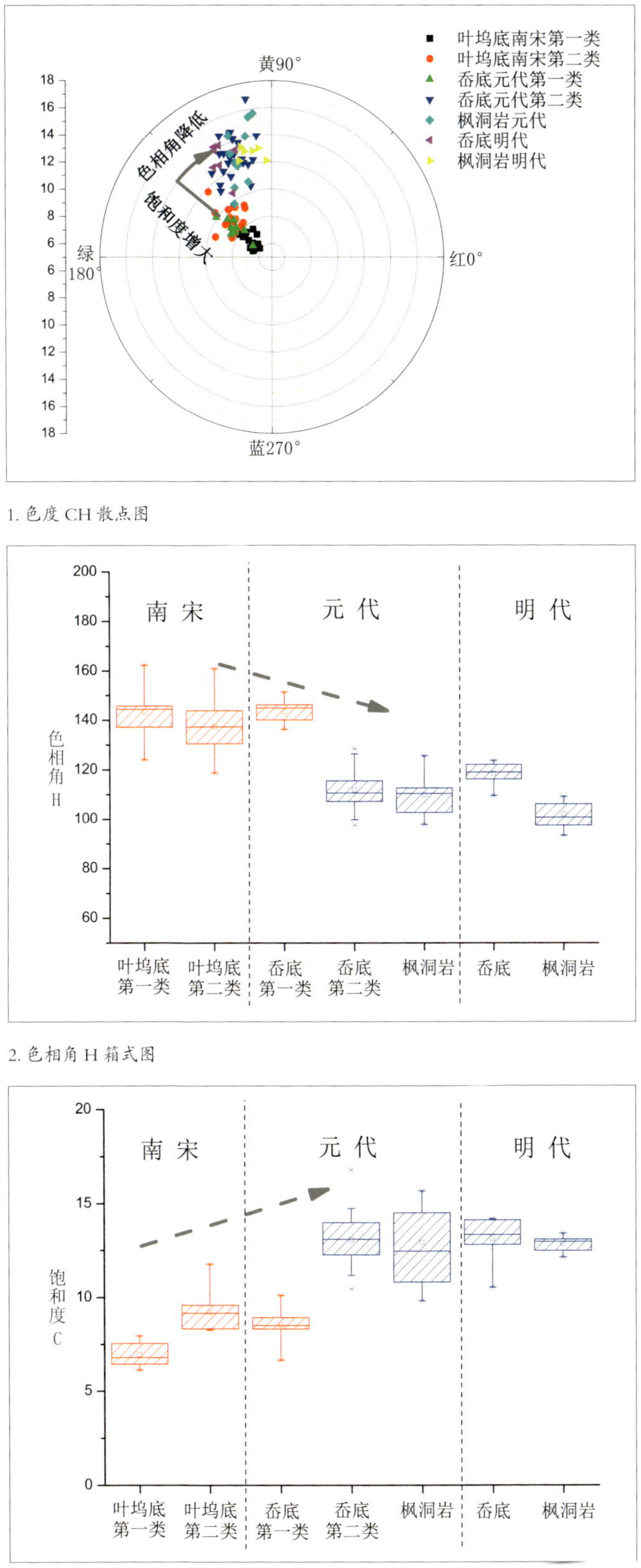

1. 色度CH散点图

2. 色相角H箱式图

3. 饱和度值C箱式图

图4　龙泉大窑不同类型青瓷釉面色度图

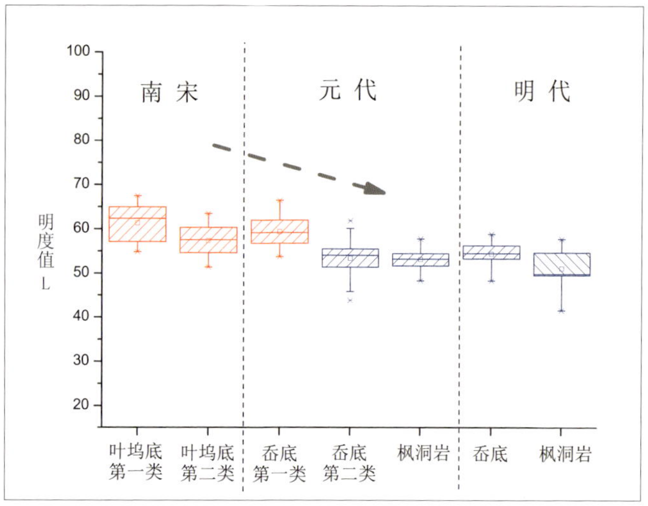

图5　龙泉大窑釉面明度值L箱式图

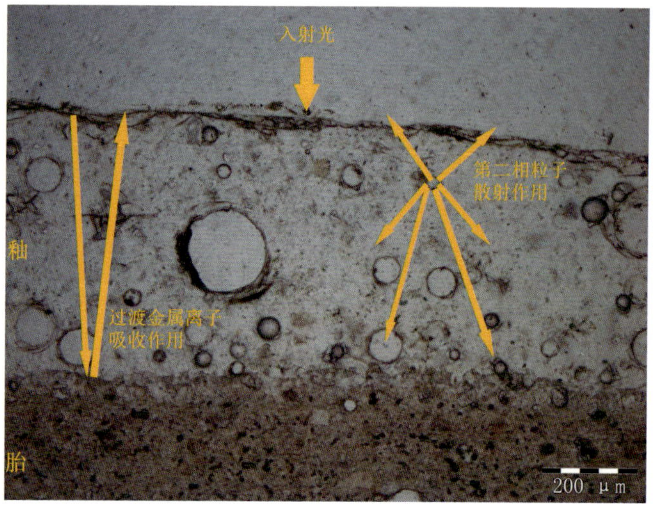

图6　釉层中吸收和散射作用

近，这一类样品釉面质量较好、釉色呈较为淡雅的粉青色。而大部分元代岙底窑产品釉色与前一类相差较大，体现在色相角偏小（平均值在110°左右）、饱和度偏高（平均值在13左右），这种色度在视觉效果上就显得较为青黄。枫洞岩出土的元代样品与岙底的第二类元代样品釉层色度坐标大体上聚在一起、较为相似。总体上看，龙泉大窑元代样品釉面除少部分还保持了南宋时期的粉青釉色特点，绝大部分釉面呈现出饱和度较高的青黄色调。

龙泉大窑明代样品釉面色度总体上与元代时期类似，呈现较低色相角、较高饱和度的特点，但不同具体窑口出土样品釉面的色相角有一定差异——岙底窑明代样品釉面色相角偏大（平均值为118°），而枫洞岩明代样品色相角整体偏小（平均值为101°）。故从色度坐标上来看，明代时期龙泉大窑青瓷样品相较于南宋鼎盛时期样品，呈现出较小色相角、较高饱和度的特点，而其中枫洞岩明代样品釉面更加偏黄。

从不同时期龙泉大窑釉面明度值箱式图也可看出与色度图（CH值）相似的特点（图5），即除少部分岙底窑元代样品釉面的明度值与南宋时期叶坞底样品相似外，绝大多数龙泉大窑元明时期青瓷样品釉面明度值都较南宋时期低。明度值反映样品的光亮程度，釉层明度值与胎体颜色、釉层厚度釉中过渡金属离子含量、釉中第二相颗粒含量等密切相

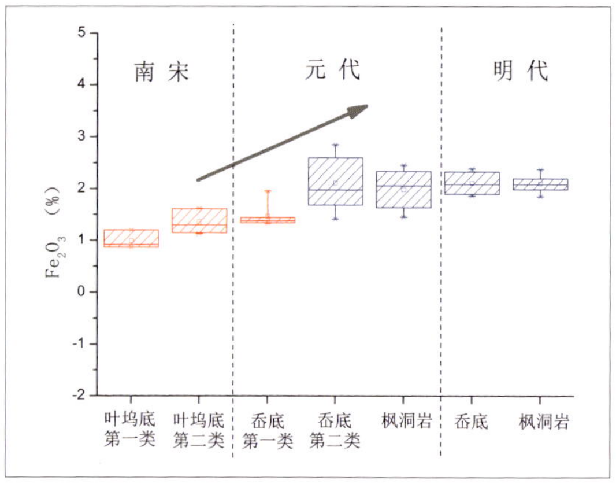

图7　釉层Fe_2O_3含量箱式图

图8　叶坞底第一类代表样品釉层断面显微结构图（100倍，正交偏光）

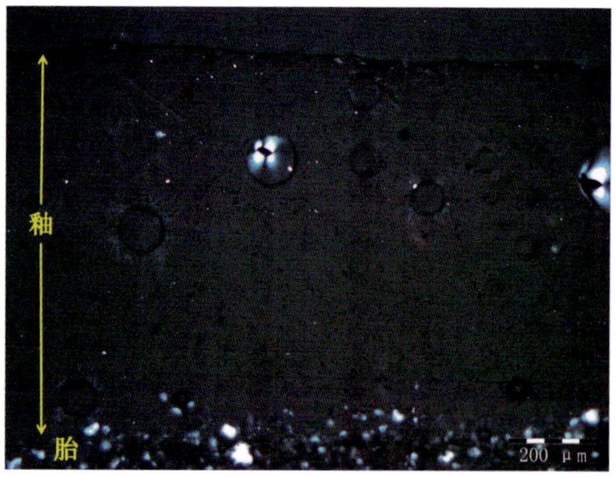

图9　元代枫洞岩代表样品釉层断面显微结构图（100倍，正交偏光）

关。从图 1 样品照片中可以看出，这一批龙泉大窑青瓷样品胎色相近，皆为灰胎，利用显微镜从断面观察可发现其釉层厚度亦较为相似，皆在 500μm ~ 1000μm。

大体来说，当外界光源照射进样品釉层后，除镜面反射外，入射光会经过釉层中过渡金属离子的吸收后，经胎体反射回到釉面；如果釉中存在第二相粒子，则粒子会对入射光产生散射效果，使入射光的一部分无法射到胎体，而直接散射回釉面（图6）。故釉层中过渡金属离子（最主要是 Fe）越多、第二相粒子（气泡、残留石英、晶体）越少，则反射回釉面的光越弱，也就是明度值越小。

从龙泉大窑釉层种 Fe_2O_3 含量的箱式图可以看出（图7），南宋时期和元代岙底第一类样品釉层中 Fe_2O_3 含量较低、均少于 2%，而元明时期大部分样品釉层中 Fe_2O_3 含量均较高，基本大于 2%。釉层原料中的铁在烧制之后的釉层玻璃体中以离子状态存在，对入射光产生的吸收作用可使明度降低。

南宋时期叶坞底青瓷釉层中可观察到较多 10μm ~ 20μm 的残留石英颗粒（图中较亮的部位）和钙长石晶体（图中较暗部位），釉中第二相粒子较多，可对入射光产生较强的散射作用（图8）。元代枫洞岩青瓷釉中包括残留石英在内的第二相粒子极少，釉层玻璃化程度较高，只可见稀少的气泡悬浮在釉中，故其对入射光的散射作用较弱（图9）。此外，南宋叶坞底青瓷釉中有较多第二相颗粒，其产生的散射效果使得釉层具有玉质感。釉层玻璃化程度较高的绝大多数元明时期龙泉大窑青瓷，釉层缺少玉质感，更显得透明。

从釉色方面来看，相较于南宋鼎盛时期的龙泉青瓷，元明时期龙泉青瓷整体上呈现一种较暗的偏青黄色，这种颜色与中国传统对青瓷釉色的审美有一定差距。元代时期，统治者崇尚白色、蓝色，宫廷对瓷器釉色的审美逐渐转向白瓷、青花瓷。加上元明时期中国制瓷中心转移到江西景德镇，龙泉青瓷产量逐渐减少、质量逐渐变差，清代时期完全停烧。至此，延续近千年，在中国青瓷史上占据半壁江山的龙泉青瓷完全谢幕。

结论

（1）龙泉大窑南宋时期叶坞底青瓷釉色分为两类，其中一类与北宋汝窑、南宋官窑较为相似，有可能为宫廷贵族而烧造；另一类样品饱和度稍高、明度稍低，有可能为普通百姓而烧造。中国唐代晚期至南宋时期的宫廷对青瓷釉色的审美倾向于稍低饱和度、稍高明度的青色。

（2）相较于南宋时期的龙泉青瓷，较高含量的 Fe_2O_3 含量和玻璃化程度较高的釉质使得大多数元明时期龙泉青瓷整体上呈现一种较暗的偏青黄色，这种釉色与中国传统对青瓷釉色的审美有一定差距，也标志着龙泉窑的逐渐衰落。

执笔人：侯佳钰　郭子莉　翟　毅　吴明俊　裘晓翔　沈岳明　史宁昌　王光尧

注释

1 中国硅酸盐学会：《中国陶瓷史》，文物出版社，1982 年。

2 冯先铭：《冯先铭谈宋元陶瓷》，紫禁城出版社，2009 年。

3 浙江省文物考古研究所、龙泉青瓷博物馆：《浙江龙泉金村青瓷窑址调查简报》，《文物》2018 年第 5 期。

4 张福康：《中国古陶瓷的科学》，上海人民美术出版社，2000 年。

5 故宫博物院等：《上林湖后司岙窑址秘色瓷的釉色特征及呈色影响因素研究》，《故宫博物院院刊》2017 年第 6 期。

6 丁银忠、赵兰、黄卫文等：《故宫博物院藏宋代官窑瓷器釉的颜色无损测定》，《故宫博物院院刊》2010 年第 5 期。

7 沈岳明：《“制样须索”龙泉窑》，《文物天地》2016 年第 7 期。

8 李家治：《中国科学技术史·陶瓷卷》，科学出版社，1998 年。

The Glazing Color Characteristics of Longquan Celadon at Dayao Kiln

The Palace Museum, The Institute of Cultural Relics and Archaeology of Zhejiang Province,
The Longquan Museum

China has a very long history of firing celadon, which has become one of the peaks of beauty in color and texture of celadon, namely Longquan celadon created by kiln workers in Song dynasty.

According to the geographical distribution of the kiln site, Longquan kiln could be divided into two major parts, the East area and the South area, with the South area of Longquan as the core, and also centered on Dayao kiln. In conjunction with the Palace Museum's exhibition *The World's Longquan of the World: Longquan Celadon and Globalization*, the paper uses spectrophotometers, optical microscopes, X-ray fluorescence spectrometer, and a large number of other modern scientific analytical instruments, to analyze and study the glaze layers of celadon from different periods excavated from the Dayao kiln, with the aim at revealing the glazing color characteristics of Longquan celadon at Dayao Kiln.

后记

从 2012 年动议举办一个展示龙泉青瓷行销世界各地的大型专题展，到现在“天下龙泉——龙泉青瓷与全球化”展览得以举办，已七年过去，展览题目的变化对我们来讲是一个了解、学习和提高的过程。

“中国古代瓷器生产技术对外传播研究”课题获国家文物局指南针计划 2012 ～ 2014 年的立项，张忠培先生和徐苹芳先生对课题的指导与支持、故宫博物院和浙江省博物馆对课题申报和后续研究工作的支持，是相关的研究工作得以按计划进行并最终举办展览的学术基础。

随着课题研究的深入，在了解海内外龙泉青瓷流布情况的同时，我们发现越南、泰国、日本、英国和缅甸、伊朗、叙利亚、埃及等国窑场都在仿烧龙泉青瓷，或者是把龙泉青瓷的文化元素融入当地传统的陶瓷生产中。对龙泉青瓷的这两种模仿，在表现形式上虽有差别，在技术史上也可分为不同层次的交流形态，但是以龙泉青瓷和龙泉青瓷文化为媒介表现的文化、技术交融则是共同的，在交融的过程中实现以陶瓷技术为代表的共同提高，从这个含义上说当时的龙泉青瓷是具有世界性的，是早期全球化的重要内容之一。故而，我们关于举办大型的龙泉青瓷专题展览的想法，也由“龙泉青瓷流布世界”转变成为“天下龙泉——龙泉青瓷与全球化”，通过展览讲述龙泉青瓷流布世界的同时，也讲述龙泉青瓷因输出开始吸纳外来文化因素，讲述窑场的分布为输出向瓯江下游的扩张，讲述海外各国的陶瓷生产对龙泉青瓷文化因素和生产技术的吸纳，讲述包括中国在内的世界各国窑场以龙泉青瓷为代表的文化交融和技术的共同提高，讲述在 12 ～ 15 世纪龙泉青瓷的时尚性和因而成为世界性的文化符号。

在开始进行“中国古代瓷器生产技术对外传播研究”课题时，关注的是中外文化技术交流的内容和瓷器的流布与海上丝绸之路的关系。通过宏观整理资料发现陆上丝绸之路沿线各国与海上丝绸之路沿线各国此消彼长的时间，正是东西方商贸、运输主线路从陆上移往海上之时，以及其体现的东西方的交往给沿线各地带来的促进作用。在取得上述认识成果的同时，我们发现龙泉青瓷文化所具有的文化引导作用，尤其是以瓷器为代表的文化交融与在世界范围内实现的陶瓷生产技术共同发展的史实，竟与“一带一路”所倡导的理念合若契符，这是最初不曾想到的。通过研究实现预期的学术目标，或者根据新的资料把研究推向一个新的高度，正是科学研究的魅力与目的。

正如王旭东院长所说，这个展览是故宫博物院“与浙江省博物馆的陶瓷研究人员在联合承担国家文物局指南针计划 2012 ～ 2014 年‘中国古代瓷器生产技术对外传播研究’课题的研究成果，但展览又不局限于课题本身”，“天下龙泉——龙泉青瓷与全球化”展览虽然是在课题研究的基础上进行的，但展示的是故宫博物院和浙江省博物馆几代学人关于龙泉青瓷研究多年来的整体成果。从展览立项到举办，先后得到故宫博物院前任院长单霁翔先生和现任院长王旭东先生的鼎力支持，娄玮副院长、任万平副院长和闫宏斌副院长多次组织协调会解决工作中遇到的问题；耿宝昌先生和院内专家一直关心该展览的进行，从大纲构思到展品的选定和断代等，都参与其中；为商借展品和展览设计等，故宫博物院很多同仁更是焚膏继晷，工作不辨昼夜。浙江省博物馆许洪流副馆长在课题立项、展览策划、各方协调工作中，一直全力支持并多方奔走，对此，浙江省博物馆同仁感慨良多。龙泉市人民政府在窑址调查研究工作中提供了诸多方便。

感谢北京故宫文物保护基金会、龙湖集团的大力支持，感谢丽水市人民政府的参与，感谢所有提供展品的单位。尤其要感谢故宫博物院、浙江省博物馆各位参与工作的同仁，以及龙泉市博物馆的相关人员，如果没有大家的支持与参与，就不可能有这个展览。

谨为记！

编者

2019 年 6 月 18 日

Postscript

In 2012, we proposed to hold a major special exhibition on the global exportation of Longquan celadon. Seven years have passed and we are now launching the present exhibition, *Longquan of the World: Longquan Celadon and Globalization.* The change in exhibition theme and title reflect our developing engagement, learning and enhanced understanding of Longquan celadon.

Thanks to support from the China's State Administration of Cultural Heritage, a Compass Project of 2012-2014 was granted, entitled *Spreading of Ancient Chinese Ceramic Technology to Other Countries and Its Impact.* We received instruction and support from Mr. Zhang Zhongpei, formerly Director of the Palace Museum, and Mr. Xu Pingfang, formerly Director of the Archaeology Institute, Chinese Academy of Social Sciences. The Palace Museum and the Zhejiang Provincial Museum provided support for the grant application and for subsequent research work. These laid firm academic foundations for us to conduct the research project as planned and to organise this present exhibition.

In addition to the global distribution of Longquan celadon, the exhibition also narrates a variety of related subjects. These include: the adoption of foreign cultural factors in Longquan celadon as a response to its export markets; the expansion of the Longquan kilns towards the lower reaches of the Ou river to boost exporting; the absorption of cultural factors and the technology of Longquan celadon in the ceramics of various other countries; the cultural merging and technological improvements at various ceramic kilns of the world (including Chinese kilns), as represented by Longquan celadon and its reproductions in various countries; and the fashion for Longquan celadon in the world of the 12-15th centuries and the subsequent transformation of the material into an international cultural symbol. The exhibition also reflects the accomplishments of research on Longquan celadon by generations of scholars at the Palace Museum and the Zhejiang Provincial Museum.

The exhibition has received strong support from the management and various departments of the Palace Museum from the time of its approval by the Museum to its eventual launch. Thanks to the support from Mr. Shan Jixiang, former Director of the Palace Museum, and Mr. Wang Xudong, present Director of the Palace Museum. Three Vice Directors of the Museum helped to solve many practical problems in the exhibition's preparation, namely Mr. Lou Wei, Ms. Ren Wanping and Mr. Yan Hongbin. Mr. Geng Baochang and many experts at the Museum contributed to the exhibition in various ways, such as drafting the exhibition outline, selecting and dating of exhibition objects, etc. Many colleagues at the Museum worked day and night on issues such as exhibition design and borrowing objects from other organisations. Mr. Xu Hongliu, Vice Director of the Zhejiang Provincial Museum, has provided unreserved support throughout the process, such as application of the research project, and curating and coordinating work for the exhibition. Various help from the Longquan Municipal People's Government made field surveys and researches of the Longquan kiln sites both convenient and efficient.

We extend our thanks to the Forbidden City Cultural Heritage Conservation Foundation and the Longfor Group for great support to the exhibition, to the Lishui Municipal People's Government for participation, and to all the organisations for providing loan objects to the exhibition. In particular, we must thank the many colleagues at the Palace Museum and the Zhejiang Provincial Museum, and related staff and the Longquan Museum. This exhibition becomes possible only because of their participation and support.

All kind support is acknowledged and remembered!

The Editorial Committee, 18 June 2019

国内借展单位

安徽博物院
北京市文物研究所
福建博物院
广东省文物考古研究所
杭州博物馆
杭州市文物考古研究所
菏泽市博物馆
景德镇市陶瓷考古研究所
江西省文物考古研究院
缙云县博物馆
龙泉市博物馆
丽水市博物馆
“南海Ⅰ号”考古队
南京博物院
南京市博物总馆
南靖县博物馆
内蒙古自治区文物考古研究所
青田县文物管理委员会
首都博物馆
遂宁市博物馆
松溪县博物馆
松阳县博物馆
苏州市考古研究所
绍兴市柯桥区博物馆
泰顺县博物馆
新疆维吾尔自治区博物馆
义乌市博物馆
中国国家博物馆
浙江省博物馆
浙江省文物考古研究所
香港中文大学文物馆

国外借展单位

英国维多利亚与艾伯特博物馆
英国大英博物馆
英国杜伦大学东方博物馆
伊朗文化遗产、手工艺和旅游组织
伊朗国家博物馆
日本东京国立博物馆
日本冲绳县立埋藏文化财中心
日本佐贺县立九州陶瓷文化馆
大韩民国国立中央博物馆
阿联酋拉斯海马酋长国政府古物与博物馆部
阿联酋拉斯海马国家博物馆

Domestic Lenders

The Anhui Museum

The Institute of Cultural Relics of Beijing

The Fujian Museum

The Institute of Cultural Relics and Archaeology of Guangdong Province

The Hangzhou Museum

The Institute of Cultural Relics and Archaeology of Hangzhou

The Heze Museum

The Archaeological Research Institute of Ceramic in Jingdezhen

The Institute of Cultural Relics and Archaeology of Jiangxi Province

The Jinyun County Museum

The Longquan Museum

The Lishui Museum

The Nanhai No.1 Archaeological Team

The Nanjing Museum

The Nanjing Museum Administration

The Nanjing County Museum

The Institute of Cultural Relics and Archaeology of Inner Mongolia Autonomous Region

The Qingtian Administration Committee of Cultural Relics

The Capital Museum

The Suining Museum

The Songxi County Museum

The Songyang County Museum

The Archaeological Research Institute of Suzhou

The Museum of Keqiao District in Shaoxing

The Taishun County Museum

The Xinjiang Uygur Autonomous Region Museum

The Yiwu Museum

The National Museum of China

The Zhejiang Provincial Museum

The Institute of Cultural Relics and Archaeology of Zhejiang Province

The Art Museum, the Chinese University of Hong Kong

Foreign Lenders

The Victoria and Albert Museum, Britain

The British Museum, Britain

The Oriental Museum, Durham University, Britain

The Iranian Cultural Heritage, Handicrafts and Tourism Organization, Iran

The National Museum of Iran, Iran

The Tokyo National Museum, Japan

The Okinawa Prefectural Archaeological Center, Japan

The Kyushu Ceramic Museum, Japan

The National Museum of Korea, ROK

The Department of Antiquities and Museums, Government of Ras Al Khaimah, UAE

The National Museum of Ras Al Khaimah, UAE

学术顾问

耿宝昌

展览出版委员会

主任

王旭东　陈水华　胡海峰

委员

王旭东　都海江　李小城　娄　玮　任万平　朱鸿文　闫宏斌　赵国英

陈水华　许洪流　蔡　琴　徐永盛

胡海峰　吴晓东　王顺发　吴松平

展览策划

王光尧　沈琼华

主编

王光尧　沈琼华

副主编

徐　巍　江　屿　吴明俊

本卷主编

冀洛源

本卷副主编

王照宇　翟　毅　刘　莹　郭子莉

展览协调

娄　玮　任万平　闫宏斌　王兆仁　李永兴　张光耀　王燕晋　陈俊旗　高　洁　史宁昌　袁　宏　吕成龙

许洪流　沈琼华　何宏斌

王　凡　黄国勇　胡武海　王　岗

展览工作组

吕成龙　徐　巍　李永兴　许　凯　苏　怡　果美侠　赵小春　韩　倩　冀洛源　王光尧　孙　悦　唐雪梅

蒋　艺　张　涵　单莹莹　王照宇　翟　毅　陈志鸿　赵聪月　董健丽　陈润民　郑　宏　李卫东　郭玉昆

高晓然　董彦卿　刘子哲　白　杨　吕韶音　周诗琪　傅梦翔　薄海昆　张倚帆　董　勃　郭子莉　武景杉

孙　洁　张玉雪

沈琼华　汤苏婴　蔡乃武　陈　芳　王轶凌　江　屿　杜　昊　陈　平　鲍亦鸥　刘晓鸿　贾国良　蒋　琳　李卫平

栾　天　胡慧媚　陈继翔　徐　莹　王　雯

吴明俊　刘　莹　裘晓翔　应　慧　沈子珍　田　力　张　帆　曾　汇

文物修复与化验

高　飞　纪东歌　杨玉洁　于子雅　雷　勇　李　合　丁银忠　段鸿莺　康葆强

展览形式设计

薄海昆　张倚帆

王　炬　李卫平

英文翻译

袁　宏　庄　颖　翟　毅　彼得·布朗　董　勃

韩文翻译

刘珊珊

日文翻译

董　丹　王丝滢

波斯文翻译

王施羽

本卷英文翻译

李宝平　奈杰尔·武德

摄影

王　琎

王旭东　蔡启华

Neda Tehrani　Nima Fakoorzadeh　Muhammad Sabir　Keyamparambil

摄像

司　冰　张云天

肖　弋　李小龙　危文翰　马倩雯　陈思敏

Academic Adviser
Geng Baochang

The Exhibition and Publications Committee

Directors
Wang Xudong   Chen Shuihua   Hu Haifeng

Committee Members
Wang Xudong   Du Haijiang   Li Xiaocheng   Lou Wei   Ren Wanping   Zhu Hongwen   Yan Hongbin   Zhao Guoying
Chen Shuihua   Xu Hongliu   Cai Qin   Xu Yongsheng
Hu Haifeng   Wu Xiaodong   Wang Shunfa   Wu Songping

Exhibition Planning
Wang Guangyao   Shen Qionghua

Chief Editors
Wang Guangyao   Shen Qionghua

Associate Editors
Xu Wei   Jiang Yu   Wu Mingjun

The Chief Editor of The Volume
Ji Luoyuan

The Associate Editors of The Volume
Wang Zhaoyu   Zhai Yi   Liu Ying   Guo Zili

Exhibition Coordination
Lou Wei   Ren Wanping   Yan Hongbin   Wang Zhaoren   Li Yongxing   Zhang Guangyao   Wang Yanjin   Chen Junqi   Gao Jie   Shi Ningchang   Yuan Hong   Lü Chenglong
Xu Hongliu   Shen Qionghua   He Hongbin
Wang Fan   Huang Guoyong   Hu Wuhai   Wang Gang

The Exhibition Work Group
Lü Chenglong   Xu Wei   Li Yongxing   Xu Kai   Su Yi   Guo Meixia   Zhao Xiaochun   Han Qian   Ji Luoyuan   Wang Guangyao   Sun Yue   Tang Xuemei
Jiang Yi   Zhang Han   Shan Yingying   Wang Zhaoyu   Zhai Yi   Chen Zhihong   Zhao Congyue   Dong Jianli   Chen Runming   Zhen Hong   Li Weidong   Guo Yukun
Gao Xiaoran   Dong Yanqing   Liu Zizhe   Bai Yang   Lü Shaoyin   Zhou Shiqi   Fu Mengxiang   Bo Haikun   Zhang Yifan   Dong Bo   Guo Zili   Wu Jingshan
Sun Jie   Zhang Yuxue
Shen Qionghua   Tang Suying   Cai Naiwu   Chen Fang   Wang Yiling   Jiang Yu   Du Hao   Chen Ping   Bao Yiou   Liu Xiaohong   Jia Guoliang   Jiang Lin   Li Weiping
Luan Tian   Hu Huimei   Chen Jixiang   Xu Ying   Wang Wen
Wu Mingjun   Liu Ying   Qiu Xiaoxiang   Ying Hui   Shen Zizhen   Tian Li   Zhang Fan   Zeng Hui

Restoration of Cultural Relic and Test

Gao Fei Ji Dongge Yang Yujie Yu Ziya Lei Yong Li He Ding Yinzhong Duan Hongying Kang Baoqiang

The Design of Exhibition Form

Bo Haikun Zhang Yifan

Wang Ju Li Weiping

English Translation

Yuan Hong Zhuang Ying Zhai Yi Peter Brown Dong Bo

Korean Translation

Liu Shanshan

Japanese Translation

Dong Dan Wang Siying

Farsi Translation

Wang Shiyu

English Translation of The Volume

Li Baoping Nigel Wood

Photography

Wang Jin

Wang Xudong Cai Qihua

Neda Tehrani Nima Fakoorzadeh Muhammad Sabir Keyamparambil

Camera Shooting

Si Bing Zhang Yuntian

Xiao Yi Li Xiaolong Wei Wenhan Ma Qianwen Chen Simin

图书在版编目（CIP）数据

天下龙泉 ： 龙泉青瓷与全球化. 卷四, 交融辉映 / 故宫博物院, 浙江省博物馆, 丽水市人民政府编 ； 王光尧, 沈琼华主编 ； 冀洛源本卷主编. — 北京 ： 故宫出版社, 2019.12
ISBN 978-7-5134-1283-4

Ⅰ.①天… Ⅱ.①故… ②王… ③沈… ④冀… Ⅲ.①龙泉窑－青瓷(考古)－图录 Ⅳ.①K876.32

中国版本图书馆CIP数据核字(2019)第301100号

天下龙泉
龙泉青瓷与全球化
卷四　交融辉映

故宫博物院、浙江省博物馆、丽水市人民政府 编
主　　编：王光尧　沈琼华
本卷主编：冀洛源
出 版 人：王亚民
责任编辑：张志辉
装帧设计：北京气和宇宙艺术设计有限公司
责任印制：常晓辉　顾从辉
出版发行：故宫出版社
地址：北京市东城区景山前街4号　邮编：100009
电话：010-85007808　010-85007816　传真：010-65129479
邮箱：ggcb@culturefc.cn
印　　刷：北京雅昌艺术印刷有限公司
开　　本：889毫米×1194毫米　1/12
印　　张：28
版　　次：2019年12月第1版
2019年12月第1次印刷
书　　号：ISBN 978-7-5134-1283-4
定　　价：460.00元

青瓷

之最